Grateful Conversations
A Poetry Anthology

Edited by

Maja Trochimczyk and Kathi Stafford

Moonrise Press

Grateful Conversations
A Poetry Anthology

Edited by

Maja Trochimczyk and Kathi Stafford

Moonrise Press

Grateful Conversations – A Poetry Anthology
Edited by Maja Trochimczyk and Kathi Stafford
This book is published by Moonrise Press
P.O. Box 4288, Los Angeles – Sunland, CA 91041-4288,
www.moonrisepress.com; info@moonrisepress.com

© Copyright 2018 by Moonrise Press for this compilation only. All poems and essays by individual poets (c) Copyright by their authors: Millicent Borges Accardi, Madeleine S. Butcher, Georgia Jones-Davis, Lois P. Jones, Susan Rogers, Sonya Sabanac, Kathi Stafford, Ambika Talwar, and Maja Trochimczyk

Cover art © Copyright 2018 by Charles Accardi, "Lost Marbles" oil on canvas. Used by Permission. Cover design by Maja Trochimczyk. This book is illustrated with photographs by Madeleine S. Butcher, Susan Rogers, Sonya Sabanac, Maja Trochimczyk, and Ambika Talwar. All photos Used by Permission.

All Rights Reserved 2018 by Moonrise Press for this compilation only.

No part of this book may be reproduced or utilized in any form or by any means, electronic or mechanical, including photocopying and recording, or by any information storage and retrieval system, without permission in writing from the publisher and individual authors.

Manufactured in the United States of America

The Library of Congress Publication Data
Trochimczyk, Maja and Stafford, Kathi, editors
[Title] *Grateful Conversations – A Poetry Anthology* (in English)
280 pages (xx pp. + 260 pp.) 15.2 cm x 22.9 cm. Written in English.

Includes original poems and essays by Millicent Borges Accardi, Madeleine S. Butcher, Georgia Jones-Davis, Lois P. Jones, Susan Rogers, Sonya Sabanac, Kathi Stafford, Ambika Talwar and Maja Trochimczyk. With introduction by Millicent Borges Accardi, portraits, photographs and poets' biographical notes.
    ISBN 978-1-945938-22-1 (paperback)
    ISBN 978-1-945938-23-8 (eBook in ePub format)
    ISBN 978-1-945938-24-5 (color paperback)

10 9 8 7 6 5 4 3 2 1

Table of Contents

Prior Publication Credits, xi

Preface by the Editors, Maja Trochimczyk &Kathy Stafford, xiii

Introduction by Millicent Borges Accardi, xv

Part I — Workshops, 1

Workshop 1 —Writing on a Prompt, 3
By Millicent Borges Accardi (2011): "grateful conversations never had but now taking place"
    Grateful Conversations Never Had — Millicent Borges Accardi, 5
    Culver City, ICU — Kathi Stafford, 7
    The Ultimate Destination — Sonya Sabanac, 8
    The Lake of Claret — Maja Trochimczyk, 9
    The Next Flight — Ambika Talwar, 11
    Grateful Conversations — Susan Rogers, 12

Workshop 2 — The Harpist at the Getty Villa, 13
Organized by Kathi Stafford in March 2013, to see the "Cycladic Harp Player" (2700 -2300 BC), an ancient sculpture at the Getty Villa, Pacific Palisades
    Still — Madeleine S. Butcher, 15
    Harp Player — Lois P. Jones, 16
    Harp Player — Susan Rogers, 18
    Seven Strings — Kathi Stafford, 19
    Proposal — Ambika Talwar, 21
    A Song of Stillness — Maja Trochimczyk, 23

Workshop 3 —Van Gogh at Norton Simon Museum, 25

Organized by Maja Trochimczyk in August 2013. Based on two paintings by Vincent Van Gogh, "The Mulberry Tree" and "Winter (Vicarage Garden under Snow)" in the permanent collection of the Norton Simon Museum in Pasadena.

   Wild Hair — Millicent Borges Accardi, 27
   Winter in the Vicarage Garden — Millicent Borges Accardi, 28
   After Vincent Van Gogh's "Winter (The Vicarage Garden under Snow)" — Lois P. Jones, 29
   Premonition — Sonya Sabanac, 30
   Into Color, Into Light — Maja Trochimczyk, 31
   Half Summer - Half Wintergreen — Ambika Talwar, 33
   Sophie and Vincent — Madeleine S. Butcher, 34
   The Mulberry Song — Maja Trochimczyk, 36
   Mulberry — Kathi Stafford, 38
   Greenery — Georgia Jones-Davis, 39
   Café Terrace with Tarkovsky —Susan Rogers, 40

Workshop 4 — Grandparents, 41

Proposed by Georgia Jones-Davis and Kathi Stafford, 2015

   Baba —Madeleine S. Butcher, 43
   My Grandmother Danced the Kazatzka — S. Rogers, 47
   Grandfather's Ring — Susan Rogers, 52
   Emily at Auschwitz — Georgia Jones-Davis, 53
   In That Banat Land — Sonya Sabanac, 54
   A Letter to My Ancestor — Sonya Sabanac, 56
   How to Make a Mazurka—Maja Trochimczyk, 58
   Ciocia Tonia — Maja Trochimczyk, 60
   Philosophy of the Skillet — Kathi Stafford, 62
   Trail of Tears — Kathi Stafford, 64
   Vajir Dei - Minister Goddess — Ambika Talwar, 65

Workshop 5 — The Museum of Jurassic Technology, 69

Organized by Lois P. Jones, Culver City, February 2016.
    Tea with *Canis Major* — Ambika Talwar, 71
    Cat's Cradle — Georgia Jones-Davis, 73
    The World Is Bound with Secret Knots — Sonya Sabanac, 74

Workshop 6 — The Broad Museum, 77
Organized by Lois P. Jones, April 2016
    At the Broad — Kathi Stafford, 79
    Blue Venus - I, Your Witness — Ambika Talwar, 80
    The Infinity Room — Maja Trochimczyk, 82

Workshop 7 — Rivers, 85
Proposed by Maja Trochimczyk and Sonya Sabanac, 2016
    Find the River — Susan Rogers, 87
    Varanasi - Luminous City — Ambika Talwar, 89
    Shifting — Sonya Sabanac, 91
    White River — Kathi Stafford, 92
    Easter Apocalypsis — Maja Trochimczyk, 93

Part II — Self Portraits, 95

1. Millicent Borges Accardi, 97
    Here Lies the Thing I Most Desire, 98
    Faith, 100
    Coupling, 103
    Ciscenje Prostora, 104
    Only More So, 106
    Adore the Field, 108
    May You Vanish Like the Wind, 109

2. Madeleine S. Butcher, 111
    Essay, 112
    Awesome, 114
    My Seeing Eyes, 115
    Aftermath, 116

Picture This, 117
Device, 118
To Come, 119
How Do I Know Thee, John Lee? 120
Black is the Night, 121
Meadow, 121
Bonsai, 122

3. Georgia Jones-Davis, 123
Essay, 124
Safety, 126
The Indifference at the Molten Core, 128
Monumental Dog, 129
This Rajasthan, 131
Understudy, 132
The Visitors, 134
I'd Like To Travel Like William Stafford, 137
Points of Destination, 138

4. Lois P. Jones, 141
Self Portrait, 142
Red Horse, 143
One, 145
Shema! 146
Günther's Tree, 147
Trélex, 148
The Scent of Ariel, 150
Foal, 151
The Landscape of Flight, 153

5. Susan Rogers, 155
Essay, 156
The Origin is One, 157
Kuan Yin, 160
Grass, 161
First Night in Takayama, 162
Longing for October, 164
What the Trees Say, 166

Across Bridges, 169
Shiawase, 171
The Poem Inside, 172
And the Soul Shall Dance, 174
This Lotus, 175
What Returns, 176

6. Sonya Sabanac, 177

Essay: Poetry – Everlasting Moments, 178
A Magical Prayer, 180
No Man's Land, 181
Mirjana, 184
Kristina Hugging a Tree, 186
Somewhere Far Across the Ocean, 188
Shifting Balance, 190
The Last Call, 191
The South Tower, 194
Upon Listening to the Sretensky Monastery Choir, 196
The White Fields of Sky, 198

7. Kathi Stafford, 199

Essay: Tulsa Town, 200
These Bones, 202
Division, 203
Hive, 204
Blank Check, 205
To May in her coma after the motorcycle, 207
Desire, 208
Never Unlock, 209

8. Ambika Talwar, 211

Essay: Poetry of Source Within, 212
Hunger of Fireflies, 216
Golden Pear: Patience or Penance? 217
Sweet Fire Dance of Dissent, 219

Kindlings..., 221
The Waking, 223
Singularity, 225
Love: Salt of the Earth, 228
The Fragrance of Prayer, 230

9. Maja Trochimczyk, 231
Essay: Why, Write? 232
Definition: Writing, 234
In Millicent's World, 236
An Ode of the Lost, 237
On Eating a Donut at the Kraków Airport, 239
Shambhala, 241
The Lady with an Ermine, 243
On Divine Comedy and Ice Cream, 245
Repeat after Me, 247
In Morning Light, 249

Biographies, 253
Millicent Borges Accardi, 254
Madeleine S. Butcher, 254
Georgia Jones-Davis, 254
Lois P. Jones, 255
Susan Rogers, 255
Sonya Sabanac, 255
Kathi Stafford, 256
Ambika Talwar, 256
Maja Trochimczyk, 256

Prior Publication Credits

Millicent Borges Accardi's "Faith," "Coupling," "Ciscenje Prostora," and "Only More So" were published in *Only More So* (Salmon Poetry, Ireland, 2016). "I Adore the Field" appeared in *Levure Litteraire*. "Faith" originally appeared in *Sulphur River Literary Review*; "Coupling" appeared in *Timber Creek Review*: "Here Lies the Thing I Most Desire." appeared in *InterDISCIPLINARY Journal of Portuguese Diaspora Studies*, "Ethnic Cleansing" appeared in *Westerly Centre for Studies in Literature*; "Only More So" appeared in *Madison Review*.

Madeleine S. Butcher's poem "Awesome" was previously published in the *West Marin Review*, Vol. 6 (2015).

Lois P. Jones's "Self Portrait" appeared in *Poetic Diversity*, Red Horse" and "One" in *Cultural Weekly*. "Shema!" was first published in *Tiferet, and* reprinted in *Meditations on Divine Names* (Moonrise Press, 2012). "Gunther's Tree" was published in *Lascaux Review* (March 2012) and later in *Poetry Daily* (2014); and "Trélex" in the *California Quarterly*, Vol. 44, No. 1 (2018).

Georgia Jones-Davis's poems, "Safety" and "Monumental Dog" appeared in her chapbook, *Night School* (Finishing Line Press, 2015); "Monumental Dog," appeared also in *Ascent Aspiration*. "The Visitors" and "I'd Like to Travel Like William Stafford" were published in her chapbook, *Blue Poodle* (Finishing Line Press, 2011).

Susan Rogers's "The Origin is One" has appeared in *Saint Julian Press, Tiferet* and *Light on Light Magazine*. "Kuan Yin" has appeared in *Saint Julian Press* and *Pirene's Fountain*. "Across Bridges" and "And the Soul Shall Dance" were previously published in *San Diego Poetry Annual: The Best Poems of San Diego*. "What the Trees Say" first appeared in *Meditations on Divine Names* (Moonrise Press, 2012). "Shiawase" and "What Returns" have appeared in the *Altadena Poetry Review*. "Grass" appeared in the *California Quarterly*, Vol. 44, No. 1 (2018). "Longing for October" was previously published in the *Kyoto Journal*.

Kathi Stafford's poems "Division" and "Blank Check" previously appeared in her book, *Blank Check* (Finishing Line Press, 2016).

Ambika Talwar's poem "Love: Salt of the Earth," appeared in *The Tower Journal*, Spring/Summer 2013, Vol. 5, No. 3: http://www.towerjournal.com/spring_2013/index.html

Maja Trochimczyk's two Van Gogh poems were published in *Resurrection of a Sunflower;* "Definition: Writing" in *NoHo Art District Journal;* "Ode of the Lost" in *Cosmopolitan Review* 2, No. 2 (2010); "On Eating a Donut at the Kraków Airport" in *Spectrum 2, The Gift*(2015); "Shambhala" and "Ciocia Tonia" in *The Rainy Bread* (2016)., "The Lady with an Ermine" is posted in Mary Evans Picture Library, http://www.maryevans.com/poetryblog.php?post_id=7032; "Repeat after Me" appeared in *Into Light: Poems and Incantations* (2016)..

Westside Women Writers at the Norton Simon Museum, Pasadena, CA, August 2013. L to R: Maja Trochimczyk, Susan Rogers, Lois P. Jones, Georgia Jones-Davis, Sonya Sabanac, Madeleine S. Butcher and Millicent Borges Accardi. Without Kathi Stafford and Ambika Talwar.

Preface

Maja Trochimczyk & Kathi Stafford

"In the language of poetry, where every word is weighed, nothing is usual or normal. Not a single stone and not a single cloud above it. Not a single day and not a single night after it. And above all, not a single existence, not anyone's existence in this world."

~ Wisława Szymborska

Poetry is an elusive gift. The women whose work is reflected in this volume have supported each other in their ongoing writing—some of them for as long as ten years. We express our support and gratitude to all the family, friends, and fellow writers on this journey with us.

Our group expanded and contracted: some women travelled a lot, others moved away; still others had to deal with illness and pain. Yet, we continued to meet and share poems, to be an inspiration for each other, especially in "arid" creative times.

The title of our anthology "Grateful Conversations" comes from a prompt by our "Fearless Leader" Millicent Borges Accardi that was given back in 2010 to a then-smaller group. It resulted in poems that remained among the favorites of their authors. Indeed, writing and participating in a poetry group may lead to "Grateful Conversations" – filled with appreciation for different sensitivities and life-experiences, and for shared interests in the poetic craft.

During the workshops, we often had the eerie experience of bringing poems on related themes without planning this in advance. Interestingly, the "communion of minds" also permeated the critiques: if most poets thought that a line, ending, beginning or a metaphor were awkward, too wordy or uninspired – it was clear that revisions were in order.

The idea of putting together an anthology based on our workshops was born in early 2016 and it has taken over two years to assemble the materials.

We are fascinated with the diversity of poetic responses to the same prompt – be it word, image, or place. Thus, we present poems from our workshops and field trips, hoping that our readers will find their diversity refreshing. The only criterion for inclusion of a workshop in this anthology is to have at least three poems that resulted from it.

We asked poets to contribute mini-essays about their personal experience with poetry and the Westside Women Writers group. The poets selected their favorite poems for a self-portrait. Poems in this section may or may not have been presented for critique during our workshops; some poems may have been previously published somewhere else. They have been chosen with great care to represent what each poet thinks of herself – as samples of her most important work, or testimonials to the most significant steps in life journey, commemorated in poetry.

We are thrilled to reach the finish line and present to our readers poems, essays and photographs by Westside Women Writers.

Let the Grateful Conversations continue…

~ **Maja Trochimczyk & Kathi Stafford**

Introduction

Millicent Borges Accardi

Westside Women Writers Group History

The premise
In December of 2008, I imagined a group of women writers of all ages and shapes and sizes and backgrounds who were at a certain level in their writing careers:

Maybe she has a chapbook or a first book, a few awards, publications. She is serious about her craft. She is not a beginner. She has either years of writing experience or an advanced degree. She exists in academia or on the fringe, teaching as an adjunct. She may feel as if she mostly writes in a vacuum. She may have children, grandchildren or aging parents to care for. She misses the interaction of grad school or past writers groups and the rigor of being a part of a writing program or vibrant community. She wonders silently if there are others out there like her.

What was created
A community of women writers working together to support each other with strong attention to craft, to grow as writers and as people in community.

How it works
We meet once a month for two or three hours.

A week before the meeting, we send via email one poem (for critique) to all of the members who print out the work, read and make comments on the printed poems.

On the day, we meet and chat and have snacks, often discussing literary events or announcements, grumbles, upcoming readings and trips.

We read our poem one at a time aloud. Then, taking turns, we give supportive and kind but not necessarily flowery feedback. We are considerate but honest. Sincere. During this time, the writer who read her poem aloud remains quiet and takes notes. After, she can ask pointed questions (if she wants) or she can just collect the comments. There are no apologies or explanations of the work before it is read or during. We try to avoid one person monopolizing "the floor." Everyone is respectful and kind.

After all of the poems have been discussed, we plan the next month and address any unfinished business.

In recent years, WWW has added field trips and ekphrastic poetry, going to museums to write poems. We have also given three group readings as WWW.

Building A Women's Poetry Group, Way Back When

Way back when in 2003, I was ruminating over the lack of writing community in my life.

After years in graduate school, where all of my friends were writers and every party or coffee meeting was an opportunity to talk shop or share books or new work, I landed in Venice, California—living alone in a 350-square-foot apartment looking out at the beach in the distance and the drug busts, homeless folks, and gang members outside my second-story window on the Boardwalk. On a good day I looked out from my writing desk at surfers and dolphins; on a bad day, I endured the shouts and police sirens when someone was detained for carrying drug paraphernalia or tools for breaking and entering, like wire pliers and box cutters. But even then, I shared my space in Thornton Towers with a lovely crew of creative folks, willing to hang out in the hall or pop in for a cup of tea and talk about theater or art or the latest reading at the Beyond Baroque bookstore.

Then I got married and moved to Topanga Canyon. Peaceful. Private yard, the window near my writing desk now overlooking a seasonal creek and wild birds. Lovely community here, but no one I knew and no one to chat with about writing.

So, I decided that there must be writers like me who existed outside academia, who had published, who were not Pulitzer Prize winners but who also were not just starting out. Somewhere in between. So I consulted my pen pal Robert Manaster for his help. He'd been active in a writing group for years in Champaign, Illinois.

With his insights and tips, I put together the following email and sent it out into the universe. I posted it on the University of Southern California's Masters in Professional Writing Program's list serve and with a few online writing groups.

Here is the announcement I posted:

– Attention Westside Poets –

Looking for members for a small group of 4-6 poets, meeting once a month (on a weekend) in West LA, Santa Monica or Woodland Hills (Ventura border) area, sharing 1 or 2 poems in a workshop environment where writers are respectful, and kind, working as a team to help the group achieve success with writing and publication – with a particular focus on deepening and polishing craft as individuals.

Here is the premise:

I am looking for writers of all ages and shapes and sizes and backgrounds who are at a certain level in their writing careers.

Maybe you have a chapbook or a first book, a few awards, publications. You are serious about craft. You are not a beginner. You either have

> *years of writing experience or an advanced degree. Or both. You exist outside of academia or on the fringe, or possibly teaching as an adjunct. You may feel as if you write in a vacuum. You may have children or aging parents to care for. Or not. You miss the interaction of grad school and the rigor of being a part of a writing program. You wonder silently if there are others out there like you.*
>
> *What I am trying to create:*
>
> *A community of writers working together to support each other with strong attention to craft, to grow as writers and as people.*
>
> *How it works: We meet once a month for two to three hours.*
>
> *A week before the meeting, we send via email one poem (for critique) to all of the members who print out the work and read and make comments.*
>
> *On the day, we meet and chat and have snacks, often discussing literary events or announcements, grumbles, upcoming readings and trips. We read our work one at a time aloud. Then, taking turns, we give supportive and kind but not necessarily flowery feedback. We are considerate but honest. During this time, the writer is quiet and takes notes. After, the writer can ask pointed questions (if the need is there) or the writer can just collect the feedback hard copies. There are no apologies or explanations of the work before it is read or during. No one monopolizes "the floor" for any period of time. Everyone is respectful.*
>
> *We discuss the next meeting (when it will be and who will host).*

I received over 20 responses. Writers who, from their first note, seemed "difficult" — who wanted to host the first event in San Diego, for example — or who wanted to discuss fiction instead of poetry were tactfully eliminated. With the remaining group, I requested a bio and sample poems. Based on the quality of the poems, from that list I selected five people: a young mother from Orange County (willing to drive to the meeting), a semi-retired book editor, a former journalist now working as an adjunct professor, a practicing attorney who was a recent MFA graduate, and me, a freelance writer. Purely by accident, we were all women.

Also, purely by accident, the current members are all over 40.

This was ten years ago. Although we have gone through changes due to members' relocations to other states or to increased family commitments, a core group has remained from the inception of the group.

The name we adopted was Westside Women Writers. And it has been a journey of trial and error as to what works and what doesn't work. But ultimately, like Goldilocks and the three bears, we've been able to find solutions that are "just right."

~ **Millicent Borges Accardi**

Part I

Workshops

Workshop 1

Writing on a Prompt

by Millicent Borges Accardi, 2011

"grateful conversations never had,
but now taking place"

Grateful Conversations Never Had

Hamim Group garment factory in Ashulia, Dec. 2010

Millicent Borges Accardi

But now taking place in my mind.
Many of the dead were caught
Sewing garments, dresses
For Target and Walmart, tailored
Pants for upscale finery shops on Fifth
Avenue, struggling to meet the US
Christmas due dates.

Many of the dead were planning
Dinner of Bhatm, rooti or chapatti.
They were mentally preparing
A slow smooth yellow curry,
Or perhaps a soup
Made of pulses for when
Neighbors stopped by.

Many of the dead were women
Whose children sat at their feet
Collecting spare threads
And remnants
Of cloth as it was discarded.

Many of the dead made desperate
Attempts to escape, jumping
Out of windows at impossible
Heights, and yet a simpler
Choice than remaining.

Many of the dead found
Locked exit doors, as if they had
All been purposely left
Behind, to fend for themselves
To rise from the inferno, to be born
Again.

Culver City, ICU

Kathi Stafford

The tubes flow out of the old man like cords,
tie him to the planet. His son holds his hand
and talks to him, so fast it's hard for me to hear,
not sure that I know what's coming next.

His eyes are closed as he breathes under the tent.
The money he made doesn't slow the way; it's
an open ride downhill now. How much does he
know—or want to know? His gray hair

shambles its way over the pillow top. The son
earnestly recites his strong points back to him.
His ode of appreciation. The dad who made it
to most of the games and all of the wrestling

matches. He's not so young himself
these days, knows what a father wants
to hear. No mention of whippings
or closets. That's how it was for all kids

back in the day, the son tells himself.
Ivory sheets—he smooths them down

with his free hand. He forgives
his dad, He forgives him, even though
the old man never asks for grace.

The Ultimate Destination

Sonya Sabanac

Your guess was always more educated than mine,
our vibrant envisions would go deep into the night.
With the box of miracle in our hands
its scent followed us as we walked
into the warm summer night;
content as babies, we carried each other in the smile
knowing — this was a confirmation sign,
a prelude to what awaits in some distant time.

Only, for you
that time came so unexpectedly fast.

As if I was watching
a plane ascended into sky,
I kept my eyes on it,
determined not to let it go
past my sight,
but the plane melted with the clouds
and I am still watching,
small
against the vastness of an empty sky.

The Lake of Claret

Maja Trochimczyk

The scent of cinnamon and nutmeg in the air
Hot sangria in my glass, white light shines
Through the rich hue of claret, opalescent
Like my silk scarf at a California party

I savor the taste of long ago — that evening
On the lake by the bonfire heating a huge metal pot
With cheap wine from bottles marked "Wino"
In a fake handwriting — no provenance,
No *appellation controlée*

We put plums, apples and *piernik* spices
Into our *grzane wino* during that fateful
Sailing trip, spending nights under dark
Fir branches, picking mushrooms
And blueberries in the underbrush

They thrive in acidic soil fed by rotting needles
Where a pungent smell of decay and fruit lingers
Beneath prickly juniper swathed in cobwebs
Drops of moisture gather on pine bark
Striped by shadows

A handful of wild strawberries glisten
Among delicate blades of grass in forest clearings
We lose our way, lured on by their promise

Of sweetness, their carmine hue, light aroma
Brightened by sunshine

We did not talk much then, my last year
Of wandering through Mazurian Lakes
Stopping at island coves, setting camp, moving on
After a morning dive to the sandy bottom,
Scattering the fish

It was best to listen to the wind in the treetops
Pine branches whispering to each other
About the end of summer, snow that will break them,
Icicles that may kill — *grateful conversations never had*
But now taking place

Photo by Maja Trochimczyk

The Next Flight

~ after W. S. Merwin's "Just Now"

Ambika Talwar

It happened just as you said. A storm
loud exciting rumbling of last night
cleared the air for blue space: look up!

Is this a marriage: union of fear and fire,
love's abundance, or an empty room?

Like when a bird emerges from oil spill
realizes wings are heavy but voice can sing
asks for what she needs,
        perfecting herself for yours.

Like when lover emerges from rumpled bed
sore limbs that beget poems, such beauty you hear
        spring birds sprinkle sky with wonder.

Like when the child with pudgy hands places them
under your eyes for toys
        dissolves all your fatigue.

Like when windows that are not windows
open and something unseen flies in
breeze subtle as a smile,
        an almost forgotten handwritten letter.

A rushing metamorphoses in you as gratitude
settles your bones for the next flight...
        And you cannot tell what just happened.

Grateful Conversations

Susan Rogers

Everything we have we're given
in love to use in love, in grace.
There is nothing we alone have written.

We are but a conversation
of light. Through this exchange we trace
everything we have. We're given

sour and sweet, lemon, raisin
and grain to bind them into place—
There is nothing we alone have written.

We eat cakes but have forgotten
their origin. We have erased
everything. We have; we're given.

We look. We laugh. We love. We listen.
We welcome gifts we embrace.
Yet there is nothing we alone have written.

Watch sunset turn to a ribbon.
Remember honey and its taste.
Everything we have we're given.
There is nothing we alone have written.

Workshop 2

The Harpist At The Getty Villa

Workshop at the Getty Villa organized by Kathi Stafford in March 2013, to write about an ancient sculpture from Greece, the Cycladic Harp Player, ca. 2700-2300 B.C.

Susan Rogers and Lois P. Jones with the Cycladic Harp Player (2700-2300 B.C.), Getty Villa, Selfie, 2013.

Still

Madeleine S. Butcher

We listen with you
inside the wheel of time.
We wait.
It comes
like air,
a slight vibration,
a flutter,
an echo,
across time it comes,
playing still.

Harp Player

Cycladic Harp Player, 2700-2300 B.C.

Lois P. Jones

You were saved from sacrifice.
Unlike the others, weathered

and bone-broken, crushed by stones
in men's hands and gathered

for their ritual. You survived —
still aglow with Paros — the mountain

of marble where god was mined
and shaped into desire. Saved

because you were ode to their song.
Your melody still adrift

across the barley and wheat fields.
I can see your long fingers

pluck the strings as it rests
on your knees. Imagine my bare feet

in pools, spangled with starlight,
calves once alabaster

like yours. It is summer. The jasmine
has made us drunk. Grapes ripen

in our mouths. Your music finds
the place without alphabet, no history

carving a word to speak the self.
Your hand draws the moon down

to the water, drowning everything
that isn't sacred.

Harp Player

~ *for the Cycladic Harp Player at the Getty Villa*

Susan Rogers

Harpist, is it the pain that sings?
I see your harp shaped like a bow
an empty curve that holds just space—
no strings. I feel the pull and know
I share some of your history.
Near my shoulder there is an arrow.
I've carried it, bitter music
for so long, I cannot place its
source. Now I just let it play me
and hold on as best I can so
I can use it to reach some grace.
Harpist, is it the pain that sings?
Sculptor, I think you also know;
I am your empty curve and bow.

Seven Strings

Kathi Stafford

I.
Thinking of notes
yet not ready to play them.
Measures filled with silence and the key of E Flat.

Rests   static   energy
He is searching for her scent   lilac and jasmine

But she has taken it with her. The map of
His body carves memory in two. He does not have much:
An ill-tuned harp
Marble to his touch.

II.
She sits before the screen, tries to search for life and
justify her choice. Now that words have gone, she
waits for sound to push her sharp and hard.

III.
Third movement. The royals lean back in their seats,
Wait for the first note. His solo grim and final, like a rake
Thrown down in a Zen garden.

Who knows where
The curve of note
Will come from next?

IV.
Notes take silence.
Art takes black.
Healing asks for
Breath, air, patience.

V.
Selah.

VI.

Maybe he's tired from last night's banquet.

VII.

The soundbox on his thigh,
Resting while he waits
On the chair of her pleasure.

Proposal

Ambika Talwar

Am a poor man's harpist.
Stars are my notes —
I sit on a four-legged
rocky bastion of love.

I shall not sink nor swim
but pluck notes that wiggle
like tadpoles stringing
in lake above your head.

Your toes wish to dip
in winding Styx, so you long
to become immortal.

That, too, I am.

Am a silly misshapen
toad on a toadstool.
Look through this frame;
stars are my notes.

I sparkle as do legends
you sorely wish you
could become — Smile away
divas into a camera.

Stay frozen while I play
my destiny in your silence.

Am a poor man's harpist:
Will you marry me?
How about a honeymoon
in the Aurora Borealis?
I will adore thee both
twice and a trillion times more…

But stars bashful and drunk
on mead milk and music
ran away in a wink of an eye.

A Song of Stillness

> ~ *for Kathi Stafford and the Cycladic Harp Player*
> *at the Getty Villa*

Maja Trochimczyk

His back tensely arches
Over the harp, its strings gone
All color bleached out of the marble
He plays chords in the air

The memory of music glides
Through corridors of centuries
Narrowing with each gesture

Non omnis moriar — Not everything dies

He smiles gently, strumming at the edge of abyss
Day after day, chord after chord
Sounds reverberate from antiquity into now

The hands that carved his hands – long gone
The audience of stone halls of Mycenae – forgotten
Their names, deeds, loves shrouded in darkness

This brittle figurine remains

Before Pythagoras (his monochord broken)
Before Dionysus's ecstatic harp
Before Orpheus made the stones swirl
Into the grandest halls of Greek isles

This song enchanted the beast, stilled
The lion and the lamb resting together
On the ledge, under the soft rain of arpeggios
At peace with the wind, with themselves

Day after day
Chord after chord
In clear mountain air
Above the ocean
Above the clouds
His music —
Silence

Workshop 3

Van Gogh at The Norton Simon Museum

Workshop organized by Maja Trochimczyk (August 2013) to write about two paintings by Vincent Van Gogh, "The Mulberry Tree" and "Winter (Vicarage Garden Under Snow)," in the permanent collection of the Norton Simon Museum in Pasadena, CA.

WWW poets at the Norton Simon Museum, August 2013. L to R: Maja, Susan, Lois, Georgia, Sonya, Madeleine and Millicent.

Wild Hair

Millicent Borges Accardi

Yellow mustard moss, green white
Gray lines.
A blue box learning
Up against the tree
Or perhaps a leather
mail bag
Near by.
Each stroke, a finger
Print,
A pushing back
of thick
Paint
The curl of a brush end
For leaves
And puffs of colorful
smoldering.

Winter in the Vicarage Garden

Millicent Borges Accardi

Unclear snow,
The quick spinning
of second sleep,
Looms, prayerfuls, sex.
It is what happens in the middle
Of the night when peasants
Wake up. Protected tasks
Precise tending in candle light.
The garden inside their wits
Clearing, a path of grey sky,
Brown trees, muddy snow.
The life and death of peasants
Remains forever the same.
Withering regularly, gone
Like heat in a smudge pot.
A shawl, here, a shovel
and then there
Is digging near the wall,
As if it were spring
and time
For a fresh quickening.

After Vincent Van Gogh's "Winter (The Vicarage Garden under Snow)"

Lois P. Jones

You said the life of a peasant
remains the same
withering regularly like grass

in the churchyard
watched him dig for hours
in the hard ground

as you painted beneath a sky
without mercy
standing so long

in worn boots
your toes turn to stone
vanish like the spinning wheel

beneath your canvas
you are still part of the scene
not yet snowmelt

but the hard month as obelisk
alive in the paint
below the few scalds of fire

as if death were a neighbor
you'd become acquainted with
the way winter removes its necessary distances

Premonition

~ inspired by Van Gogh's painting "Winter (The Vicarage Garden Under Snow")

Sonya Sabanac

A long, rough, brown wall
with the snow on the top
separates the city
and where you are now,
but it makes no difference to you.

This city in which you lived and
engraved steps in its streets
it's just one dark, big smear behind.

The winter days give in to darkness
so easily. Those few people who came
have said their last words and rushed
back to the distant orange light.

They left you with this man in black
the same one whose shovel
you heard times and times again,
its agonizing sound
made you cut off the ear.
To no avail, this man is here,
casting the frozen dirt on you.
Once he is done,
only the barren trees would remain,
skeletons of life that once existed.
Occasionally, the wind would break the silence.

Into Color, Into Light

> ~ after Vincent van Gogh's painting at the Norton
> Simon Museum, "Winter (The Vicarage under Snow)"

Maja Trochimczyk

Board the train from Paris to Avignon,
Flow through landscapes in TGV comfort
Move from the opal grey mists of urban rain
Into the intense fantasy of color and light
You never thought existed

Scarlet roofs, violet fields of lavender
Gold sunflowers turning their dark faces
Toward yellow eye of the sun in the azure
You have never seen such phantasmagoria
Of hues, far beyond of what you could imagine

*   *   *

Now, you know why you have to stop
At the threshold of the museum, frozen in place
By the flaming branches of a mulberry tree

Now, you know why it is so hard to listen
To the song of the old man bent down
Beneath darkening winter sky

> *the shovel, the shovel,*
> *the shovel, the snow*
> *It's heavy, it's heavy*
> *it's heavy, it falls*

You look across the hall at the grey.
Soft snowflakes at dusk, helpless
Against the darkness of bare soil
Trees covered with a blanket
Of wet snow, precariously balanced
On the blackened limbs of winter

A man has to do what he's told to do
To eat, to earn a cot in a cramped room
In a soot-covered hut

the shovel, the shovel
the shovel, the snow

Darkness and light
Night and day
You know why,
Now, you do
Know why
This longing
For freedom

Half Summer - Half Wintergreen

~ after Van Gogh's paintings: "Mulberry" and "Winter"

Ambika Talwar

O Mulberry, while you rise in curves from gilded Ground of Being,
curls and swirls and swathes of grass celebrate each other;
Shadow of self looms high into beneficent sky, purple potent indigo.

Your cousins in winter field witness a worker quiet as cold-green sky
raking snow-clad earth. What is Man thinking? Listen to his breath.
He keeps clearing hard land. For what? Food? Coins? Penance?

His black clothes dim the walled field; horizon lies beyond borders,
where desires arise – Invisibly. A hint of air … and then dissipate.

Wall is mute and cold — *sans* warm colors: tomato, radish, beets,
or butter — But sun-gold tenders your roots curling in darkness;
ochre, umber, sienna pull your feet into the wet soil.

Let us dance, O Mulberry, a dance as silkworms that feed on you
make thread, while Old Woman hoary, naked, her dugs hanging
like her chin spins beneath our feet, the snow, the grass, mulch.

Listen to her hum – a rumbling *Sagezza* – hymn to love what awaits us.
Her discordant rhythm caught in winter dread and summer's passions.
Surprise weaves my naked skin: half summer, half wintergreen.

I quiver between my two same desires: ultimate union, ultimate
cessation. Spindle, spool, woman's fingers pull the wool, and Time,
huddled in a cave, leaps into our arms, plucks our strings,
…skips away to all our continents.

Sophie and Vincent

~ after Van Gogh's painting "The Mulberry Tree"

Madeleine S. Butcher

It could be that this mulberry tree
is low enough for a child to climb
for a fine hiding place
to survey her domain
of far hills and reaching fields.

She might hide from her nurse
who is calling her name,
a wee figure almost gone - past the long fields —
her white apron flies up like a miniature flag.

And so this child becomes part of a branch
so still she is, sitting above
in the tangle of limbs
under cover of leaves
waiting for her friend in their mulberry tree —

with his satchel of chalks and charcoal and pens
who sits by the trunk in his wide-brimmed hat
fingering his pastels, ruffling the paper
and slowly, he too, grows quiet and still,
gazing out at the fields and the following hills,
their silent domain.

The afternoon moves along
to the swirl of leaves and buzzing bees,

the soft grit of chalk, the scratch of pen
the heel of his hand blending sky to earth
wind to cloud, branch to leaf —
fields and sheltering hills.

The afternoon moves along with the sun
and an occasional shiver of limb and leaf
as mulberries are picked and many are eaten
but most are dropped in a perfect lazy rhythm,
down straight down on his wide-brimmed hat.

The Mulberry Song

~ after van Gogh's Mulberry Tree at the Norton Simon Museum

Maja Trochimczyk

I am the mulberry tree, ablaze with color
before the last day of autumn

I came into being in a flurry of brush strokes
on a cardboard, under the azure expanse of unfinished sky

turquoise — into cobalt — into indigo
green — into chartreuse — into amber — into gold

buds into blossoms — into fruit — into earth
to fall — to fall not — to end — to end not —

to begin

The brightest star, an ancient supernova,
I am aglow but for a moment

I outshine reality with artifice
exploding off the canvas

paint — paintbrush — swansong

leaves of the earth — ripples in the stream — crystals in the air
aflame, all aflame

I make magic of the
mundane shape of the world

sic est gloria mundi

it is — it will be —
it is willed to be —

once captured in a frenzy of light,
becoming time

transfigured into swirls of awareness
crystallizing at the edge of oblivion

I am the mulberry tree —
I am the alchemist tree —

let my song fill your day till it glows —
become pure gold with me

Mulberry

Kathi Stafford

There is no blue without yellow and without orange.
~Vincent Van Gogh

The branches flare out. They'll go so dead
in winter that one will think, *What can come back
from that*? But Lazarus arms surge unbound
in spring. Now the surface blurs orange and yellow,
purple fruit hidden in the air. A cauldron whirls

Deep beyond the woods. Mitten-shaped leaves
paw what the bark stands down, as an autumn
brush heads to closure. What can arise from
this consistent loss? A plain mystery shows itself
in the roots, twisted, Medusa hair swirling

Asps into the cold air. The tree collides with night,
stars and all. Fence posts built from the Mulberry,
haphazard in night air. Fruit   bark   hues
blaze in a bounty. I hold them in my hands
as well. Precious are the stripes of the wounded tree.

Greenery

Georgia Jones-Davis

You are no gardener.
You water and clip,
hopeless with squash,
tomatoes, anything floral.

It is leaves you love,
pine and rosemary's needles,
basil's aromatic ovals,
oregano's delicate, draping chains;

nervous rustling of the sycamore
whispering of departure;
 tenor chorus of oak and laurel
when the wind kicks up.

A tight-fisted, bright green bud
bursting from the walnut's limbs —
sheer adolescent hubris,
a shoot aimed straight

at its own papery heart;
the leaves,
green and gold, bloodshot
or brooding brown,

the way they turn
their plain, veined faces
toward the sun
in widening hope.

Café Terrace with Tarkovsky

Susan Rogers

The tables are empty
because we ate all the blue food
at Café Terrace.
Still hungry, we polished
each plate clean — flung them
into air, spinning stars.

Some descended into
tabletops. Some fell
and turned to cobblestones.

I fell into my glass of wine
and became the night.
You drank from my glass
and disappeared into rain.
Rain merged with fire
and all the colors began to burn.

Cobblestones are fish swimming
in streets. Doorways
are barns swimming in fire.

The sky is pierced with sonnets
swimming in dark water,
each one a hole of light.
Follow them across the river
of our conversation.
Constellations of poetry ignite.

You and I converge in blue lines.
Night is a lullaby that carries rain.
The tree sings.

Workshop 4

Grandparents

Proposed by Georgia Jones-Davis
and Kathi Stafford, 2015

Madeleine, Millicent, Sonya and Kathi in Sonya's garden, 2016.

Baba

Madeleine S. Butcher

Angel wings of white linen
folded long ago between tissue,
a child's pinafore
with butterfly sleeves
seem like a dream
found in the great wood chest
she is quietly closing
listening for her grandmother's steps.

The third floor beckons
the grandchildren to ride
the forbidden narrow bannister face down
to resurrect the unknown child
who had fallen decades before them.

The conservatory is warm and wet in the winter
and fog covers the glass —
palms, orchids and ferns fill
this place.

The rock on Baba's mantle
is from the old Boston Opera House
torn down in 1958.

The leather bellows is cracked
but still works to fan the fire.

On foggy nights the fog horns
call to each other.
'Pray for the fishermen', she says.

Baba is spooning mashed potatoes
from a bowl held by Anna,
as though they were soft cement
and require a firm hand.

Anna came into her household
from Ireland many years ago
when she was sixteen.

It is a rule to say hello to Anna in the kitchen first thing when you get there.

"Hey kid, are you the kid who knocked the kid around the cornah kid, cause if y'ah kid, I'm gonna ring ya neck, kid"
is her greeting to us.
We blast around her kitchen shouting
she chases us out.

It is a rule to always stand up when an adult enters the room.

She, her granddaughter,
is the only one named for her,
though they are embarrassed
and avoid this fact.
She is counted but not seen
in the small army of cousins.

COLORFUL FACTS:

<u>Baba</u>
Never missed the opera or symphony
Reliable on a two-man saw
Raised money for Albert Schweitzer
Spoke on the phone with Jackie Kennedy
Turned Episcopal later in life
Harnessed her own horses
Once had lunch with Woodrow Wilson
Grew up with no penicillin

TIME: Decades later
PLACE: Haight-Ashbury

My mother calls
"Baba died last night."
Oh, Mum.
"In her sleep."
Shall I come home?
"Heavens no!
 It's going to be a madhouse."

"She said 'let the grandchildren come
and take what they want.'
They'll be taking numbers
like at the bakery. All 14 of them,
13 without you."

I'm on the phone, it's a dream,
it's a long distance call...
Baba, is that you? Static roars.

"Yes, dear, it is I," she says.
"I just wanted to say good bye…good bye."

She says this in her musical voice
almost as though she's saying "Hello."
Almost as though she's surprised
to be able speak into this amazing device
and to talk so easily to someone
from such a great distance.

Photo by Madeleine S. Butcher

My Grandmother Danced the Kazatzka

Susan Rogers

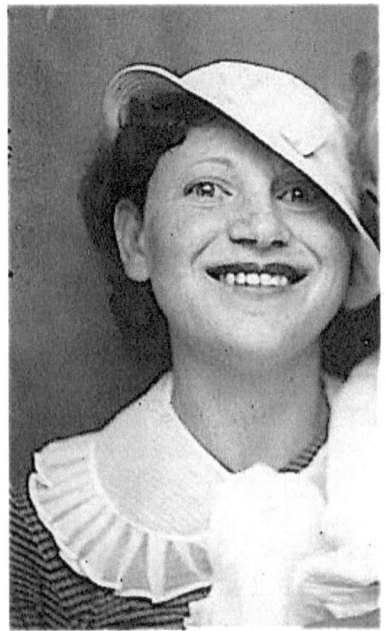

Photo of Rose Rogers

Ninety
was her life's goal.
But life's more than numbers.
Feisty Russian, she kick-danced till
the end.

The end
was the river.
They took money in shoes,
few objects on their backs. All eight
waded.

Weighted
with water, soaked
beyond repair, money
lost to the river, they labored
for bread.

For bread,
for just one loaf—
her brothers worked all day.
But when they sliced it open, found
maggots.

Maggots
inside the loaf
but resilience inside
their hearts. They went to bed hungry,
dreaming.

Dreaming
of the new world
across the sea, she learned
to say "Past sixteen." Practicing
each night.

Each night
seemed strange to her:
English sounded crazy.
But she could speak words she needed
to work.

To work
in this great land
of opportunity
was blessing. She grabbed for jobs like
apples.

Apples
in their orchard
near Kiev would ripen

so fast, her whole family picked
all day.

All day
in this new land
she brought the red sweetness
of Russian apples to her life
and danced.

And danced
with her new friends
and with her man, as bride.
She danced Philadelphia to
L.A.

L.A.
became her place
to root. Three children grew.
Even there, when her boy got sick
she danced.

She danced
bubbling up joy
enough to share with each
open heart she met, spreading cheer,
sunlight.

Sunlight
filled her life, sweet
as beet soup, wild as rose.
It was her gift to make people
happy.

Happy
even when she
almost lost her child, and
when she did, she walked the streets for
money.

Money
to honor him.
She collected each day
donations for City of Hope,
small coins.

Small coins
can add up fast,
like the years, one by one,
until the bank of life is full,
brimming.

Brimming
with love, she gave
everything away, so
easily: strudel, jewelry, clothes
pictures.

Pictures
show her smiling
in costume, pregnant bride.
She enjoyed the joke, the laughter
given.

Given
to embellish
it wasn't always clear
when she was telling the truth, yet
it was.

It was
after all hers.
Her life, her tale, her way.
At the end, she was almost there.
Ninety.

Ninety
years was her wish.
She was eighty-nine. Was
it so wrong to embellish, sing
for her?

For her
she was ninety.
In the hospital room,
we sang, "Happy Birthday, Grandma,"
and danced

and danced
around the bed.
Her eyes smiled at the thought.
She could almost see the balloons.
Ninety.

Grandfather's Ring

Susan Rogers

Kicking off your shoes you ran laughing to the water's end.
Trailing paths of sand and shells, I followed.
At first touch the ocean circled around our hands.
Your eyes were amethyst flecked with gold.
My ring was violet in the April air.

I lost my ring in the water
where for a moment I could see it
glinting like a purple star.
Then the water took it. You told me
I'd always know exactly where it was,
but nothing stays just where it falls.

Now several Aprils since, you are gone,
the ring and the white space it left on my hand.
I see oceans too circle back to touch the shore.

Today, in the too-cold shallows I glimpsed
a piece of abalone shell, petal-shaped, white,
with a rim of purple scalloped round
like the slender lash of an eye. I reached for it
through water so clear I could almost see my smile,
and missing only shell, grasped everything.

Emily at Auschwitz

Georgia Jones-Davis

She wore the thin
leather boots bought in Haight-
Ashbury. On the ride
back to Kraków
a disturbance crept up on her,
a disturbance she could not recognize.

Joseph, her great-grandfather,
arrived in one of the last transports,
never left.

Does blood murmur to its own
through ash that still dirties the air,
bone whisper to its own
through dust piled beneath the soles?

In this place where the dead survive
did Joseph's fire-eaten eyes
know Emily on sight,
the daughter of his daughter's daughter,
a link in the dying chain

miraculously alive.

In That Banat Land

Sonya Sabanac

Long ago, before I was even born
in the far away flat land of Banat
where wind scatters the dust
and rivers lazily flow

      my sorrow was conceived.

In that same land, my great-great-grandfather
grew grapevine and believed
no animosity was stronger
than a glass of good, old Banat Riesling
drank with the salute for good wishes.

      The bullet did not care what he believed in.

His son, Zhiva, "muzikant,"
was the first violin at weddings and village fairs.
When fertile Banat fields delivered,
his music would praise the Autumn
and override the echo of Hapsburg Monarchy's guns,
but a "dying beast" needed new blood.

      Zhiva played his last czardas on the Hungarian bomb

leaving my grandmother a pitiful
nickname that in whispers followed her
with its sad sound like a funeral march,
"posmrche" — a child
born after its father gone.

But that was not enough!
The second big war froze the Banat fields
one desolate night,

    my grandmother's second born had to go.

Different uniforms and languages,
marched the land of Banat.
For four years, a boy, who would
become my father, dreamt of a day
his father would come back home.

    In 1945 an unknown alcoholic man, claiming
    to be his father, came to stay.

Forty seven years later,
at the time of blood and betrayal,
I sought refuge in that land,
but I forgot what I should not have,
my grandmother's genes in me
would repeat her fate,

    my second born has passed away.

The pain made me run,
run so far away,
determined to break the curse of that flat land
I hid my first born in the New World,

    I let her cut the ties and become
                            someone else.

A Letter to My Ancestor

Sonya Sabanac

I was always curious about you,
but I don't even know your name,
I can only count
three generations back.

To learn about you,
I imagine myself
where you lived.

Banat of Temeswar,
The Habsburgs' Military Frontier
and ever changing 19th Century,
where one could fall asleep in
one and wake up in another country.

How much of a good fruit
had fallen into your lap?
Your hands always nursing,
the land or the babies,
must have wanted
to fly away sometimes.

Did you lie in a grass
and travel with the clouds
when the lust for going far
would fill your heart?

And what did you do
when darkness fell
upon your world?

Frozen winter nights,
vagabond soldiers appearing
out of nowhere…
My brave ancestor mother,
you secured a passage
for me to come.

Distance of time
is between us,
but I feel you are not far.
Come into my dream and
tell me what I want to know
most of all,
what is yours that I carry on?

Photo by Sonya Sabanac

How to Make a Mazurka

~ after Chopin's Mazurka in A Minor, Op. 17, No. 4,
 for my Grandparents, Stanisław and Marianna Wajszczuk,
 who could play and bake their mazurkas like no one else

Maja Trochimczyk

Take one cup of longing
for the distant home that never was,
one cup of happiness that danced
with your shadows on the walls

of Grandpa's house, while he played
a rainbow of folk tunes
on his fiddle, still adorned
with last wedding's ribbons

    mix it – round and round to dizziness

stir in some golden buzz of the bees
in old linden tree, add the ascent
of skylark above spring rye fields,
singing praises to the vastness of blue

    mix it – round and round to dizziness

add Grandma's walnuts, with
chopped figs, dates and raisins,
pour in juice from bittersweet orange,
freshly picked in your garden

mix it – round and round to dizziness

add dark grey of rainclouds in Paris
that took Chopin back to the glimmer
of candles in an old cemetery
on the evening of All Souls' Day

mix it – round and round to dizziness

bake it in the cloudless heat
of your exile, do not forget to sprinkle
with a dollop of sparkling crystals,
first winter's snowflakes at midnight

Ciocia Tonia

*~ for my Mother's Aunt, Antonina "Tonia" Glińska,
deported by the Soviets to Siberia in 1940*

Maja Trochimczyk

Only a pear tree
between fields of sugar beets and corn.

Ripe pears — that's all left from the house,
barn and orchard. The farm where she raised
her sons, milked her cows, and baked her bread.

Only a pear tree. A lone memento
standing forlorn in an August field.

They ploughed it over— the village church and bus stops,
the neighbors' corrals, where their horses used to neigh.
They ploughed it over — her garden of herbs
and cosmos, its fragile lace of leaves kissed
by sunlight, a dream of a flower, really —
she used to so love its ephemeral beauty,
a ghost of the past.

It was the worst, then, to see her neighbors
running with news — her husband shot
in the middle of the dusty village road.

No time for grief, she saved her tears for later.
The orders came at once: a day to pack,

a long train ride to an unfamiliar city,
near a river she never longed to see.

They said, pack wisely — take only
 the warmest clothes, boots, pillows.
Bring as much food as you can carry.

Where you are going, there is nothing,
except for freezing breath
and bitter cold.

It is not painful now, just surprising,
her whole life gone, and only one tree left.
No trace of her ancestral village on the maps.

Only a pear tree
in an empty field of stubble.

Only a pearl tree
in her golden field of dreams.

Philosophy of the Skillet

Kathi Stafford

She and I never saw eye to eye especially
In the kitchen   where we held to
Different world views

Edna believing in
Accumulation   great shelves crammed
With fennel seed and forbidden rice

Cans of French green beans and artichoke
Hearts   Gumbo with okra and
Shrimp she'd tossed in that morning

Held with her philosophy of the skillet
Season it girl   she'd tell me while she
Looked out over her tomato plants in the back

Now played out and shriveled up
Just like her   *Don't scrub that pan*
You'll ruin it if you keep it too clean

Me the nun of scrubbery
We will go to the bottom of grit not a
Kernel of corn left   no drop of oil

Like the grief I've bent over for years now
But it's getting me nowhere   man
I tried to rub it loose like gravel

On the lake road   so let it all
Build up   dear Auntie   I give away
My rules   these very strict rules

Grace for the dirt   that's what I finally
Say as I start to shrivel too   ready
For the redemption of the skillet

Photo by Madeleine S. Butcher

Trail of Tears

Kathi Stafford

"I fought in the War between the States and saw many men shot, but the Cherokee removal was the cruelest work I ever knew."
~ Georgia Soldier

She has walked three hundred miles but will walk
No more. She passes in childbirth and leaves
Wenona, Firstborn Daughter, my grandmother,

Five times removed. The name of the mother
Might be Adsila, the Blossom, or Woya, my Dove.
Her thin back wavers on the trail

Above the aqua blue beads she has sewn
In her moccasins. *Nu na da ul tsun yi.*
The place where they cried.

Tie the shells to my ankles. Dance west
East   north   south, while
The water drum and the river cane flute

Finally sound out our mourning joy.
Hear trumpets and rattles fly above
The hum of shaken gourds.

Paint the sky blue   black
Red   white   the Cherokee colors
in every direction, above, below, within.

Vajir Dei – Minister Goddess

Ambika Talwar

LEFT: Ramma Talwar (Mama), Vidya Prakash Kapur (Nana-Pitaji), Uma (Shanti) Kapur (Nani-Mimi), and young Ambika Talwar. Right: Vajir Dei.

You are Vajir Dei
So briefly I knew you at 4 or 5 years — I cannot forget.
With natural love of a great-grandmother in *salwar-kameez*,
you would fuss us to sit; your face head covered
with a *chunni* is clear in my eyes.

Then you would get busy by a stove
you would roll *parathas* in seven layers
with *ajwain* seeds and salt

spread *ghee* in each layer, then roll again
before you placed it on the *tava*
Before us would appear bowls of savory *aaloo*
malai daal with *raita, chutney, chaaval.*

You would feed us delicacies of a lineage long forgetting

we whose roots were torn shattering like rooftops
lanced by heartless ways of war. *Not our war.*

Aya Ram Dhawan, our Baoji was getting older.
I was just two feet off the ground. He would rest his feet
on a *palung* a cot of coir woven on a 4-legged wood frame.

Vajir Dei! You had Nathu, Shanti, Kunti, Raj, Krishna,
Jaswant and Darshan: 4 daughters and 2 sons.

Your daughter Shanti became Uma, my nani, my Mimi.
Promised to my nana when she was but a little girl
and he a boy. How family ties were sanctioned.

They were noble. Nana-Pitaji was an engineer
in the British army as you know —
an officer in the war to end all wars. *Not our war.*

Mama watched her masi Krishna die of typhoid.
Mama said your sister Rukmini lost her husband
in the 1947 riots: he cried for freedom.
Their son, shattered at this loss, disappeared.

Films show us wretched breaking of ancestral homes.
Pigeons would burst like flames into sordid skies.
Guns and pellets made thunder. Stealing of brides was a norm.

Pinjar: skeleton, bones.

I have wondered what parts of me are come from them.
My papa's idealism feeds my dreams of familial unities.
Childhood lost to his nana's rigid ways, mother's neglect.

His poetic pulls in me to restore innocence to broken

worlds – *shayari*, couplets he used to recite eyes aglow.

Vajir Dei, you left your home with two-three articles of clothing.
How tied we now are to all that we own.
Pitaji was gone to Iraq for that war. When he returned
India was quartered in pieces: wars spilled over pavements,
through doors. Water wells filled with dead people.
Birds of prey wild with intoxication.

Mimi had left with her two girls. Pitaji came later...
No one knew if he would. In the exodus, he was careful.
Who knew who was of which side: He could have been
killed by a barber's knife. Life was this fragile,
caught in a trick of a thread's unraveling
or a syllable a sound a stick a name.

Pinjara: a cage.

I cannot imagine how you lived through such fires
you who left everything for refuge in a broken capital
in your own land — what is it about mad men who start
a war to end a war but which never ends? How can it?

They are still fighting one land, another, and then another.
Has it been a conspiracy for 1000 years? *Not our war.*

Was I not born in a hospital built for the wounded?
Of the war that nana went to? Same war hasn't ended.

Vajir Dei! Mama said in those days girls were named like this.
Vajir is a minister. *Dei* is *Devi*, goddess. Bhabhiji!
You are Minister Goddess. Those seven-layer *parathas*

can feed an army. Let us feed the army so well that
jawans have enough savory skeleton and mass to return home.

Gazillion gazillion tears have fallen and risen into gardens.
Let us name a flower *Vajir Dei, Uma, Ramma….*
Imagine Sargoda, a pond, filled with *chameli gulab, mogra.*

Once there was land of five rivers where our people came from.
Now we are scattered spores… roots, weaves, *dholki* and song.
I have a *khes* woven with threads, the kind you used to make.

Photo by Ambika Talwar

Workshop 5

Museum of Jurassic Technology

Workshop organized by Lois P. Jones in February 2016 at the Museum of Jurassic Technology in Culver City.

Tea with *Canis Major*

Ambika Talwar

Canis major reigned on a sofa in new tea room gilded with old art curving lines of café frosting, windows of muted light… dust of time to never be hurried by fake moon or any act of chaos.

My eyes lingered over a teapot on a rust plastic tray… In wonderment, my gaze flitted between long snout and regal air whose glance shook me back to the red room with portrait of dogs — but this *Canis* budged not a bit — and woman with lucid gaze in long gingham-like dress.

She smiled at me, offered me tea, while *Canis* looked at me matter-of-factly.

I said, "No…er, thank you." They were all smiling at me. There were three.

Then I said, "Actually, yes. Black, please." "Namaste," she said. Room was filled with smiling. With a Georgian air, she said, "We give you Indian tea, no milk."

I asked of her origins. "Georgia," she said, including her friend with auburn locks.

In the kitchen was the third caretaker, creating film to record eccentric tones.

Astonished, I felt I entered this room on a time machine.

Not one but three women spry and cheerful – eager, warm, and courageous.

Canis major budged not a bit but sat sprawled, content to let the Milky Way course around his swirling gait furry, grand, resting.

I called him *Sirius* — for his exquisite poise was as mysterious as it was commonplace.

The girls posed for a photograph, suggested I take stairs to the terrace.

Here, pigeons coo at one another, look at me askance. Love endures in broken places. As if time doesn't mean anything... a small fountain plays its game under sun-trickled grey-blue sky.

Sublimation is like this: that a solid substance is rarefied — the city is no longer as it might one day... no sound of the ardent traffic. Nothing.

When hearts stop beating, even footprints dissolve
Nothing is. But point of light swallows darkness. Whole.

Cat's Cradle

Georgia Jones-Davis

Mother and daughter, we played cat's cradle,
never understood in those rare
peaceful moments between us,
how we had entered holy ground,
entered, yes, say it, the web of all being,
the ties that bind us;
entered Spider Woman's sacred weave,
a marriage knot, sailor's knot, Windsor knot,
knot of whale-gut, understanding naught,
the tangled rooted knots of the human tree,
the placenta knot of maternal blood bond,
James Bond's Algerian love knot,
the knots in the wood that forever fuels
the cremation fires of Varanasi,
the cradle of ash piles
where holy cows and pariah dogs
wander between the pyres.
Thou shalt not.
Cat's Cradle — soft finger tips pulling taut
as instruments — sitar, dobro, viola, lyre,
thread or gut or cotton string,
tight as the cloth we weave,
will wind ourselves within,
shrouded in knot, nada, nod, naught,
garlands of memory and *moksha*.

The World Is Bound with Secret Knots

Sonya Sabanac

I found an unexpected garden on the roof!
This Moroccan-style garden
with the ornamental blue tiles,
carved wood tea table, lavish plants,
the soothing water sound from the fountain
and most of all, the mourning doves
makes me feel as if I stepped into a parallel dimension.
The mourning doves' cry transports
me back to a different
age and place, for their cries
are both for eternity and passing of life.
Against the law of physics,
I am at the two places at once,
in two gardens.
I am eleven years old again
and reading a book at the sun.
Through the lines I hear a dove's cry
and I travel through my blood stream
to that place of our past.

Below this Moroccan garden, there is a house
taken out of time, full of mysterious
holographic codes and images
coming from the mind of "Master of a Hundred Arts,"
a man who wanted to reveal
the law by which the world runs.
An inventor, composer, historian,
geographer, adventurer.

And again I think of you. That
whole place looks exactly like you.

For in your own way,
you too were a Master of a Hundred Arts.
I am convinced
your zeal to know so much,
your undying desire to learn the secret,
made you go so soon.
As if you have chosen
to be only a man of the 20th Century.
That was your stage on which you paced
up and down in great performances,
so admirably self-assured!
No Passaran!

The world is bound with secret knots,
so here I am, in this surprising garden
unsure if this was a dream.
Perhaps you will appear as one of
Kirchner's holographic images
right here in front of me to couple
with the mourning doves' cry.

Photo by Ambika Talwar

Workshop 6
The Broad Museum

Organized by Lois P. Jones, April 2016.

L to R: Maja Trochimczyk, Sonya Sabanac, Kathi Stafford, Lois P. Jones, Susan Rogers and Ambika Talwar, 2016.

At the Broad

Kathi Stafford

When I was born, they thought
I was a lark. Twirled among tall trees.
First, dove to the dirt floor of the hidden
Forest. Tunnels lie beneath
These woods. The first time I got
Trapped there, my bird heart beat so fast
I thought it would fly out. I ran into the wall and
Blacked out.

I whistled through the
Maze, all purple and blank,
When I work up. The inner
Curves of me flashed up out
Of hot darkness. My head, black and
White, my feathers, red and yellow.
I'm no blue jay or
Parrot. Light bounces
Off my riffly chest.
Joy wings high.

Blue Venus — I, Your Witness

Ambika Talwar

Sweet Sapphire Flame, once wild,
wilder you are now. With tensile
strength, you stand gloating broadly.

Madly, I witness gorgeous blues
of your thighs to be loved
as in a temple with high walls
layered with susurration.

Pleiades sagely dance your body.
I walk around you — an inspector.
You lift to your eyes your wanton dress
crumpled in time's Kelvin freeze.

I love the stars in your hair
you plucked as a child. Sirius B
you saved for a future lover —
Where is he? This erring human.

A fiery blue pillar poised glistens
by you. What of bowl of white crocus
for Narcissus listing in moonlight,
willful beloved — adoring servant?

What fires burn in your womb?
O Blue Venus, what loves weave
your skins with shades of song?

Do your curves love water
skin-to-skin kissing muscle, ligament,
hair, elbow blue with rhapsody?

O Gift of Vision! Your thrilling blues,
your wandering ways, your lustrous eyes.
What does your body say about
mine stitched with life's bruises?

I shall lose nothing ever again.
I shall keep you in my amber eyes!

The Infinity Room

Maja Trochimczyk

At the Broad Museum, is closed, as they say.
I do not trust them, anyway. I would not go in.

I find my own infinity on the beach —
floating on the waves that cross the Pacific
to lick my toes covered with sand crystals.
It is scattered among multicolored pebbles
in shallow tide pools I walk through to reach you.

I'm home now.

My infinity stirs in dewdrops on the grass —
diamond sparks on moss green, chartreuse and celadon,
shining in early spring light.

It tastes refreshing in cold juice of an orange
picked in my garden when it is 33 outside. It echoes
in the melodious phrases of the mockingbird
that claims the top of my pine, its contours
outlined against the misty hilltops
and the bluest of California skies.

Where is yours? Where have you found
that spark, that voice, that calling?

Is it in the sunrays bouncing off the mirror surface of the lake,
splitting into a myriad prisms between your fingers —
your private rainbow? Or the hot desert wind
that challenges you to a race across sand dunes?

Maybe you walk into the white expanse of the museum
filled with a bunch of Jeff Koontz's metallic balloons
and see yourself reflected in the smooth, polished skins,
bright and translucent like air bubbles, a giant child's delight?

I hold a bouquet of infinity in my hand.
It opens to blossom in ellipses, circles, petals —
intersecting trajectories of light, reverberations
of energy reflecting a multitude of timelines —
crystal after crystal — wave after wave —
carnelian into amber into gold — emerald into sapphire
into quartz crystals — sparkling above a multitude
of mirrored cupolas — other infinities that pass me by.

Photo by Ambika Talwar

Photo by Maja Trochimczyk

Workshop 7

Rivers

Photo by Lois P. Jones

Find The River

Susan Rogers

It happens on occasion.
The rain falls in a sun-bright
sky. A perfect watercolor
landscape bleeds. An unexpected
fountain forms where
a pipe has ruptured

on the ground. The unthinkable
occurs. Not the impossible.
Just the unplanned,
unanticipated, out of the blue.
It can happen here.
It can happen to you.

When you least expect it.
You might be walking
down a familiar street,
some ordinary afternoon
and a passerby will say to you,
"Pssst. Come over here.

You cannot walk on this road
anymore. It is not open for you."
What are you going
to do? When the rain falls
in a clear sky, you may feel
a note of wonder. You

may smile even though
you suddenly get wet. When
a red rock in your watercolor bleeds,
you may have the chance to picture

a novelty: a brilliant scarlet river.
And when you come across

a broken pipe, you too
may break into release,
into a rush of buoyant water.
It goes both ways.
You may choose to see
inconvenience

in the rain,
ruin in a watercolor,
loss of water in the geyser.
You may choose to regret
the unforeseen, yet
why waste your limited,

extraordinary breath?
It happens on occasion—
the death of a bird too small,
after it plummets
from your backyard tree.
The place you have always

known as home pretends
you are a foreign country.
What are you going to do?
It's bound to happen.
I suggest we slip
into another view.

Choose a new street,
look through our difficulty
and see the unwanted, differently.
Start now. Find the river
in the bleeding rock,
the beautiful singularity.

Varanasi – Luminous City

Ambika Talwar

Banks of ancient Ganga sing of before and after life;
ash and saffron flowers float, syllables sink to river
bottom amid silent wailing, ripples passing by.

One hundred meters away, funeral pyres release
violent flames, which disappear into crows' azure.
Thus legends lie still or vanish, but story of Shiva
is endless even if partly forgotten. Memory needs
not quietude... Walls are gouache of spit images.

Daily bathers cross the river, dip in its cold currents
as I did one winter morning with my father, while
mother and companions watched from a little boat
rocking in its karmic rhythm, stories of scriptures.

Sangam of Varuna and Assi, Shiva's luminous city calls
golden time of respectful order to lift us out from
anular confines, bitter nuance of broken columns,
houses of fussed music, sweet aroma of betel leaves,
as heart-full romance of beaten souls wander.

I write these words: city streets winding as mothers
in rags ache for fulfillment, not lost in hunger
nor destitute as mountains strip-mined of essence,
as rivers sinking into oblivion, as plants whose sap
forgotten lingers in glance of Mother's tears. *Ghajini*
posters on walls as cows die for plastic foods.

Despite this shattering, Varanasi smiles, sentiments
like incense swirls rises into clouds calling rain

in spring. May these be woven in silk, for gentle curves
of Parvati's bruised shoulders under an old banyan tree.

Bones of the burning dead float freely in fast currents.
Do not drink this water! Let dead dreams dissolve.
into liberation. Let them not haunt the living...!

Photo by Ambika Talwar

Shifting

~ for Lana

Sonya Sabanac

Like a water-lily whose root
was plucked out, you are barely
floating, detached
and fearful —
your world has collapsed.

The time has not come yet,
but one day, one morning
you will wake up and find out
that a blue sky is enough.
All the sadness that you soaked in,
all the torments have changed you,
you are no longer ignorant.
You came to know the pain,
but you also learned
how everything moves and shifts
how we could be safe in transitions
as well. After all,
we are like rivers running home.

White River

Kathi Stafford

Ozark Mountains   three am
While we float down the White River
My dad shushes me *You'll scare the trout*
But I'm only seven   braids down my
Back   as my hand trails above a
Whorl of leaves

Sweetgum   cedar   redbud
Dogwood   the trees that will
Show up when dawn does
White oaks tucked into the hills

Gray and blue curves bending low
Into water line   the decisive flick of a
Guide's wrist   who will get you on the
Fish   brown trout hides
Beneath the hum of water

A tenuous dam where copper coins wink
At me in profound silence
I admire the flow   the quick whip
Line into depth

And later a fire where filets will
Simmer up in the shape of summer

Easter Apocalypsis

~ after "The Discovery of Heaven" by Harry Mulisch

Maja Trochimczyk

It is coming. The angels know.
They dwell in their Piranesi castles,
twisted spaces where outside
is inside. They are not indifferent.
Not too smart for their own good.
Not cruel. They don't tell us.

The end is coming, it is near.
Not death, mind you, not that
ugly spinster without its twin.
No. The end of the end. *Finis.*
The satin fabric of a wedding dress
trails behind the veiled beauty
as she glides towards her beloved.

The river's end tastes of salt
in its own mouth, opened widely
into the waves of the ocean.
Nothing we can do will stop it.
Just stretch your fingers,
let the water cool your skin.

Why resist? Heraclitus
dipped his toes in this river.
Shape-note singers praised it.

Saints dove in and swam around,
luxuriating in incandescent glories
that passed us by.

The end is coming, flowing
swiftly down the slopes.
Let's sit on the porch, doze off
in honeyed sunlight,
before it, too, disappears,
transfigured.

Let us believe there will be
light enough inside us
— that kindling of kindness,
 a half-forgotten smile —
to keep us afloat in the final flood
coming, coming to erase the world
and remake it, anew,
bejeweled.

Photo by Maja Trochimczyk

Part II

Self-Portraits

Millicent Borges Accardi

Here Lies the Thing I Most Desire

Unnamed, as familiar as Pao Caseiro,
With its seven cups of white flour,
And variegated sea salt greyed
On each crystal at the edge of my hand.

Here lies the thing I most desire
The active dry yeast waiting in its
Plastic container in the fridge,
Inside the nest of what it can be.

In my mind, the chemical reaction
Is already exploding like love
At age 12 when it is ripening
And distant. I see the sugar
Combining and bursting
In a foamy cup of hot water, mixed

With orange juice,
The milk of adolescence
Also waiting to reach room temperature.

Here lies the thing I most desire,
Mixed with a spoon until consistent
And predictable. A life you can shape
And let rise and then pound down
A second time until it is comfort-soft
And feels like old fabric.

Here lies the thing I most desire.
I let it rest and bake and turn

Golden until I tap it and hear
A hollow sound.

Photo by Madeleine S. Butcher

Faith

At night the careful hands
of nuns tuck underneath poker-faced
hips, and braid spirals. Spurious
dry fingers comb, wrap around,
and memorize a lost art.

They rock quietly against the mattress
and dream of things
they will not do.

Outside the cloister
a milky statue of the Virgin Mary
stands. Arms

collected,
face cast down, shielded by
Botticelli's wreath; under half lids
stony, rambling, the eyes breathe.

The marble skirt encloses other eyes,
petals too. While faithful prayer-sitters
speculate humidity,

the pedestal's scalloped
edge embeds Mary's feet
in Venus's half-shell.

From inside the white-washed convent
    the inhabitants rush to
genuflect in disinfectant and soap.

    Too fluid
  for focus, they stop, now
  and then, to gaze through
    the thick third floor
curtains at the statue below

  where Sunday children touch
Mary's stone breasts and place
   potted roses at her feet,
     wishing, wishing.

  As young girls, nuns nodded
  God's halo around their hair
and lit single candles. When the mother
  superior lifted their veils
  she offered wax for sealing.

    After the benediction,
      like the newly
      dead, nuns don
      solemn white.

   The only other color
they ever wear flows onto cotton
     rags between
     their thighs.

This stale aired extra room,
 this end of a knot,
 this jump into frozen water,
this daughter waiting for words,

 every month,
it requires this cardinal leap of faith
 for them to still
  believe
  they
  are
  female.

Photo by Madeleine S. Butcher

Coupling

The woman thought she would be good,
making sure he washed,

rescuing black stockings, wood pile
scraps. Finding theatre tickets

and collecting parking stubs.
She thought she would be good

at using his soap. Remembering
not to wear perfume and waking

up to call home. In the hotel,
hiding while the hot water ran,

her heart compact as plywood.
She thought she would be good

at belonging. The bulk of her time
a two-by-four dove-tailed into a corner,

getting the best he had to offer.
She thought she had a talent for being aloof.

On him, she made few demands.
When he was away, she imagined

his heart open, fearless
hands holding a piece of wood steady
while a diamond-point blade cut through.

Ciscenje Prostora

(Ethnic Cleansing)

This woman does not know he
carries the devil's four poster bed
in his palm, clutching it like promised
money: Bosnia, Croatia, Serbia, home.

She can't predict the hour
he will climb the steps, laughter
echoing behind him, his boots
scraping the stone, his steps
following her mother's call.

She only knows that the rebel tanks,
with nudies plastered to their sides,
are rolling through her town, shaking houses
like wind, carving up the patterns of the land.

She knows not to stare back
when he finds her, hiding behind a clay
pot. When his soldier's eyes become her
life, more understandable than her or me or any
pronoun she whispers out between no and help,
she shuts her eyes, imagining cold weather.

He tries the rug of her family's house
with the slant of his hips, dragging
her shoulders along behind him.

Her skin beneath his, now
this skin that he uses for the rhythm
of bodies, now pushed up against
a wall, this skin he now needs, this drumming beat,
this having nothing to lose.

Serbia, Bosnia, Croatia; the countries undulate
together while he dances the dance of the basilisk
thighs marching, marching.

Even little sounds, like birds overhead,
encourage him to go on, to spit, to breathe
three generations of her surrender into his lungs.

Then, silence.
Lost territories, rebels, food, clothing, shelter,
she thinks not of peace, but of surviving
the winter, of outlasting the enemy, of winning.

Only More So

You see it was very much like this.
In the flatland dregs, the fat-coated
soldiers knocked at the door, so a woman
was forced, with a gritty smile,
to invite them in, to sit by her
yellow fire, to swallow up her walls.

In the corner her husband rubbed
a wooden rifle, tapped wooden boots against
a wooden floor, thinking, thinking
visitors are cold as bad luck.
He looped his fingers under his belt
and turned to gravel.

The soldiers, making circles in the dust
on the hearth, asked the woman to remember
the unremembered: the jewelry sold for food,
the Moravian lace curtains.

Where are the rings? Two and now one?
The woman spun her wedding band around her
finger and gave them her best,
"we were here before you" silver glare.

Surrounded by dust and half-opened words,
the woman's mottled eyes brought a dull patina
to the repeated questions. The sharp wool collars
of the soldiers pointed south; inside,
the crudely made benches evaporated into firewood.

It was like this: the woman's hips swayed
like harmonicas when the men watched her fetch
water and run it into the basin, cracking
ice with her fingernails.

They asked her, Why do trees mean? and
What does water stand for?
while their stares mocked the broken
windows, and pain, itself, counted the woman's
buttons as they easily slipped through the stitching
of her clothes.

You see it was all so simple:
they wanted the smooth golden of her neck,
the warm nest of her skirt;
her loss shifting like daggers beneath their skin.

As wind fragmented, as doors burned,
as fires latched, the last woman, this last
woman, clasped a bowl to her chest knowing, knowing,
what the snow outside pretended, knowing
that nothing important ever belonged to her.

That now she must survive by owning air,
holding back the red, the full, the bare,
the proud canvases of flat language paper
that once told her everything she needed
to know.

It was like this, only more so.

Adore the Field

~ *translated from a blog by Jacinto Lucas Pires*

Many times I, by hand,
Over hand, imagine shades
Of the finished trees
Wrapped up for the soul
Both black and white
Stepping over plants
With their spotted-rooted feet
as if they were Helen of Troy.
Oh, how many times not
Did I desire a garden of where
To plant steel and other hard verses
of the sky filled with an immensely blue
Size that we only can have
When we are far from the city.
And also I see, in the paintings
of António Palolo. Oh, the space.
The holes in the landscape,
Bare places-palcos, where we can
Sing. To dance, to speak when the world
Stops masking the face of modernistas,
Stops glorifying saints, olharapos rags
Clothes or threads, futuristas, no,
Not, that, I adore the field.

May You Vanish like the Wind

It wasn't real to me, the king who had a daughter
Whom he dearly loved

And how will I find you without a map?
The troubles that come with old age

Almost never require me to attain more
Power and I said the princess dressed herself

Every day and combed her hair as if it were a dense
Garden of residence. Her thoughts led her through

The windmill and placed her on top
Throwing stones at the dirt below which
Reminded her of childish freedom

As a voice of her father her mother and the servants
Combined into one, she took leave of the palace.

She thought that his voice, the voice of her prince
Should come for her like the softened wind of summer.

As it always did. She tucked her hair behind her ear
And listened for the prince who said, "Go and call me"

The next day the voice at the same hour as the day before,
Came for her and she rose to meet it like a visitor at the door

And the voice took her through the air, placing
Her on the banks of a slow river where washerwomen

Were scrubbing clothes. In one chorus the women called out,
May you vanish like the wind. May you vanish like the wind.

Photo by Madeleine S. Butcher

Madeleine S. Butcher

Essay

Language was always a lively subject growing up in our house. Grammar, spelling and phrasing were questions debated and explored.

Writing was also encouraged and for my 7th birthday, I was given a pink leather diary with a lock. Correspondence with my sister, who had gone away to school, kept her vital presence in my life and then, always, the writing of the endless thank you notes that my mother insisted be written with originality and sincere gratitude.

After years of being a dancer and actress, I began writing monologues and short stories. Merrill Joan Gerber guided me to be part of her home writing group, Logos.

In 2001, I got married, moved to the West San Fernando Valley and met Millicent Accardi when she came to my Pilates class. She suggested a writing challenge called "Poem a Day" and suddenly poetry became an express train to a new language that bore a powerful and unexpected translation to my ideas.

Westside Women Writers is a beautiful group of accomplished and developing poets. They are a force of encouragement, education and support.

~ **Madeleine S. Butcher**

Photo by Madeleine S. Butcher

Awesome

Awesome has taken on a daily feel
as in — "I'll have fries with that."

Our waiter writes it down, nodding.
"Awesome," he says looking up.
"Anything else?"

That awe...

as in feeling so small
before a thing so vastly greater than we,
a thing embodying a profound truth
which we can sense but not ever truly know,

...should be applied to an order of fries...
is a thing in itself of great wonder and incredulity
which often but not always
stands side by side with
incomprehensible idiocy
laced with such sweetness
that one feels oddly and deliriously hopeful.

My Seeing Eyes

So many years I wouldn't love my mother —
I lived in other cities,
never telling her anything real.

She waited for me, decades passed,
she married again, took care of her husband,
busied herself with her other children. She knew
not to come after me, though she held me close
as though folded into her sweater drawer.

She called me B.J.,
she called me Little Lu.
She made me eat my peas and beans.
All of that and more than I will ever fathom.

I first opened my seeing eyes to her
and she was smiling at me in her soft blue sweater
cradling me in her arms, rocking,
and light shone all around.

I tried to live an opposite life from her,
looking for the least familiar face.

When it finally turned around she was still
wearing her soft sweaters and loved to watch the birds outside.
She looked at me, unable to speak, unable to walk or stand.
I was the child who left home and she was my mother
who had held me here in this life.

Aftermath

My eyes are bathed in light,
illuminated in muted reds
my comrades and I
are stilled in the aftermath of intermission.
We've been barely spared
from too much beauty —
stunned
by an invisible blow
to the chest —
we are left wondering
what to do
what to say
how do we go on?
Do we pick up our purses and coats,
and walk away?
Do we not?
Do we breathe?
How do we go on
from this splendor?
Are we to be left alone
with only ourselves
to pick up our shattered remains?

After Paul Taylor Dance Company, "Airs", Los Angeles, 2014, Dorothy Chandler Pavilion

Picture This

I couldn't be more surprised than you
to find myself writing, not reading
poetry of all things.

Oh sometimes reading
the ones who rhymed —
the school book poets
who bored me in high school
like insects tacked to a board,
writhing and squirming
weirdly alive like forced blossoms.

Someone blew the top off —
don't know who!
But up it comes
in your face —
listen to this

picture a road and cows —
the earth seen from space —
an Airedale at the edge of town —
the snowplow before dawn —

I'm talking to you
I'm telling you things —

picture this.

Device

This world
this invisible world
of long white corridors,
silent except
for faint white noise —
clicks, distant tapping —
a hum of distantly placed fluorescents.

This world
takes quick delivery of the mind
transmits at the speed of light
a brief thought from our companion

who has dropped away
is now a dry husk
we are alone in a vast field of tall grass
that sways from a passing wind,
trees at the horizon
a floating moon above.

Photo by Madeleine S. Butcher

To Come

She floats on a wide, slow river of contemplation —
burnt gold leaves fall into brittle piles,
shoes scuffle the sidewalk,
the dark shining wood of her school desk,
a strand of hair tangled in a button,
a bob white's call —
intimate friends, boys, books,
family suppers, seasons,
all held in the keep of her mind —
each detail of her ordinary, wondrous life
comprising the golden riches for what is
and what is to come.

Photo by Madeleine S. Butcher

How Do I Know Thee, John Lee?

He lies blinking in the dark
his eight-year-old self, listening to crickets,
to the creak of his bed,
to his parents' whispers on the other side
of the slatted wall
and he hears his papa say —

*he's got the boogie-woogie in him and it's got to come out —
yes he does,* says his mama, *yes he does.*

His hands reach into the dark
he spreads his fingers —

the night lifts the ceiling off,
he sees plowed fields fall away,
a path into shining woods he's never seen —
he lies so still he hears his heart
beat his moving blood in the midnight darkness.

His heart so old and young
looks back from the night
light spills in from the slatted wall
his parents' whispers
and he feels — *so good, so good* —
*so much more than that share-cropper's cabin
can hold in all the world.*

Black is the Night

Black is the night
in the Grand Canyon,
steep is the trail.

Gone are the batteries
in our $1.10 flashlights.

We claw our way up,
feeling the perfect
silence of rock,

the perfect
indifference of time,

and the complete, perfect
idiocy of our lives.

Meadow

How the field lies
under cobalt skies
the great gaff-rigged pine grove
at its mooring nearby.

Bonsai

I will stop time for you.
I will live in your time.

I will search for the molecule
That makes you the way that you are.

I am outside of you
But I live inside of you.

You are your own miracle.

I will shrink myself into the size of a pea
And sit by your mighty trunk
To feel your understanding of things.

You draw children in to you.

You make us wish for the same
Miracle that you are.

Photo by Madeleine S. Butcher

Georgia Jones-Davis

Photo by Neil Gruen, Gruen Photography

Essay

When I took a poetry workshop in college, I did not find community. I found a brilliant but high-strung poet professor and a roomful of insecure, morose, dark-haired, grunge types — this was more than twenty years before the grunge scene brought to you by Courtney Love and Kurt Cobain. It was a mean-spirited lot, not encouraging, quite terrifying actually. I froze up like a blended Margarita. Meeting my professor at his office hour one day, he said to me: "What has happened to you? You can't write an ounce in this class."

I returned to poetry a few years after college when I met and studied in a workshop with a wonderful poet who was a former newspaperman. (I don't remember the mild group very well, but for one member I'd gone to school with who stayed a long-distance pal and eventual Facebook friend.) Our fearless leader soon moved out of town, I joined the staff of his newspaper and tossed all poetic ambitions overboard.

My writing life blossomed in the newsroom. For the first time, I met people passionate about the importance of the written word in a way that felt truly grown-up. I concentrated on journalistic endeavors — profiles and interviews, book reviews and criticism. My prose grew lean and literal. Poetry and its vagaries were banished.

After I left the newspaper world, poetry timidly came back to me like a long lost, beloved dog, muddied, starving, and in desperate need of good trim. This is when I discovered how supportive, critical and fun a poetry writing group of peers can be. In the seven years I participated as a member of the Westside Women's group, I could see how all of us were lifting each other up and along, each individual voice receiving the editing and feedback needed to shape it into more of itself.

Group readings and literary chat over lunches were a delight. Field trips to museums were indulged in. Books and chapbooks were encouraged and published.

It took relocating to another state to end my regular participation. I do miss this group of gifted, honest and mature poets and the support and wisdom they share.

It's funny, I will refer to myself as journalist or an editor, but I don't feel comfortable calling myself a poet. I don't wear those poet's blouses or long black capes. I don't hang out in coffee houses anymore or try to look poetic or grungy or depressed.

I tell people that I like to write poems. A day when I have a poem in the works is a happy day. Whole afternoons are gobbled up in the joy of working with language, building something.

Ideas for poems are often stimulated by what I am reading at a particular time. A phrase will itch. I will have to write it down and see where it takes me. I am not an occasional writer. I cannot command a poem into being.

As with newspaper editing and writing, I know when I've done good work and when I have not. Poetry has taught me, if nothing else, how to be completely honest with myself as an artist. There is no cheating in poetry or art. There is only writing the best that one can write. When a poem is completed and I am happy with it, I will celebrate — a walk with the dog, a glass of wine. But the celebration is brief.

The next time out, I will have to do the best work I can do all over again. Yesterday's news is yesterday's news. Or on the bottom of a birdcage, as journalists like to say.

~ **Georgia Jones-Davis**

Safety

After the funeral of a great aunt,
distant cousin, old family friend,
my parents would take me
to the steakhouse with tartan wallpaper
and quilted, red leather seats.
We would slide into a cool, secretive booth
of burnished wood,
fold our hands on the rustic tabletop;
manhandle the great mug of salt
or pepper grinder with its metallic crank,
and breathe in the aromatic gloom.
Meat was cooking.
You could hear fat sizzle.
People happily murmured
in the darkness around us.
The knives and forks were weighty and large,
the napkins thick, rough, white squares.
Meat was cooking.
You could hear fat sizzle.
The newly dead person
was not ordering a T-bone.
The dead person was alone in a box,
in blackness.
We would eat, my parents and me,
not saying much,
our heavy flatware clashing,
swords in battle
on the wood, plank plates.

On a night like this,
there was no tomorrow.
We shoveled in buttery, salty potatoes
baked in their earthen jackets,
browned as if still dirt crusted,
potatoes that tasted
of the sea, far away,
and of loamy soil.

The Indifference at the Molten Core

The road to Sendai
flaps like a fish
the sea swallows its tail
four trains vanish
Fukushima Daiichi fails
we wake
to a radiated night of rain
that we prayed
had scattered into shadows
on a wall in Hiroshima
and the *Hibakushas*
evaporate again
in wave after wave
the drowned drowned
in the white flotsam
of our industrial order
cats and grandmothers wash ashore
a curled seashell once a small boy
barnacled to a door

Monumental Dog

Where is the dog the Soviets
shot into space in 1957?
Where is Laika tonight?
Her bones could be sailing overhead,
a satellite of the cold war
stuck in the traffic of the commuting sky.
Experts now contend
she died of overheating
within hours of launch
because her R-J sustainer failed
to separate from the payload.
She died,
the rest of us believe,
an orbiting, kenneled cosmonaut,
a terrified dog star,
night and day chasing past her,
the moon escaping fast as a cat.
She howled, I am the only dog
circling the campfire of the world,
lonesome as a wolf
in the prehistoric shadows.
On the sixth day her breath evaporated;
She starved and froze in her capsule
as the human sounds she recalled —
"moya malishka, moya Laylika" —
receded in her ears
with the memory of meat
and Kremlin bells only a dog can hear.
Laika was mailed into space,

a letter never answered,
a missal to the gods of the future.
To please him she submitted
to her handler's velvet-voiced commands,
the same voice that whispered her name.
She thrilled to the clammy, cushiony hands
that stroked her fur
even as they strapped her in.

Photo by Sonya Sabanac

This Rajasthan

For so long now
beneath parched stars,
in the Thar Desert of the Rajah's
jeweled darkness,
the pen scratches at nothings,
at lost alphabets
of loose-leaf wings,
languages elusive as the rats
in Bikaner's temple.

Against evening's ruby sky
in emerald branches
lifeless as kindling,
owls weep.
Feathered clouds flock,
rain descends, its drops
round as startled eyes.

For so long now,
Vedas and chants
for monsoons
to roar down the hazy
Himalayas
of the mind.

Understudy

Even this most glam of blondes,
always a step away from stardom,
exhales with a noisy rattle
through a thirsty mouth
on her death bed.

My Hollywood aunt Margot
is eighty-five now,
her dyed blond hair fanned on the pillow,
 a sanitized scene in a movie.

Margot used to know Marilyn Monroe.
Those girls were bosomy buds
on the ripe bush of contract players,
but only one was plucked.
Still, they often ate lunch together,
on the lot of Twentieth Century Fox.

Chewing commissary chicken salad,
Marilyn said things to Aunt Margot:
"People," she confessed,
"people see somebody else in my movies.
They aren't seeing me.
They are seeing a ghost of me."

"Those white cotton panties,"
Marilyn informed Aunt Margot,
"are for nuns, for the faint of heart.
Loose them, darling.
Loose all panties.

A girl's got to breathe,
don't you think?"

"Dying," Marilyn, over tuna salad,
explained to Aunt Margot,
"dying is not for anyone
with a fear
of performing in public.
It mostly happens anyway
in front of an audience."

We gather around Margot's bed.
This is theater, and finally,
Margot is is the star
of her own seven year itch.
The hospice nurse
checks her vital signs.
Margot hasn't opened her eyes
in seven days.

Still, the nurse deposits a tray
with a chicken leg in brown gravy,
mashed potatoes, carrots,
a little tub of vanilla ice cream.
And a small box of chocolates
and a single red rose,
curled and darkened
at its used-up edges,
forlorn in a pink, plastic cup.

The Visitors

Three horses —
two roans and a ghostly gray —
muscle across our lawn
at the first light of morning,
stop in the suburban street,
as their breath clouds widen
in cold that knifes the lungs.

Fathers in buzz cuts
shout across driveways.
We kids wake to urgent voices, commotion,
run outside in pajamas, followed
by sleepy Medusa mothers in pink rollers.

People stand frozen, electrified
by this vision —
something out of the dead time
when pathways in the tall grasses
were no wider than flanks,
three horses
in the cul-de-sac.

Bart and Scott's father
orders a posse of neighbors.
With yells, car horns, and prods —
golf clubs, butts of rifles —
they herd the horses
into a car port,

block them with a black Ford
and a red and white Studebaker,
big engines idling hot.

Bart and Scott once drew me
into their garage
to show off what it was
their father had brought home
from the woods.
In the dark I edged up
against an object

bristly, cold, suspended.
Beneath my Keds
the floor felt sticky.

They flicked on the light.
I was face to face
with a bruise-eyed buck,
shot and hanging
by its hocks,
head and small antlers swinging,
drops of its blood
on the oily concrete.

Fear for the visitors
shoot through me

until a Tesuque Pueblo man
in a blue pick-up appears,
its headlights blinding
as a spirit's eyes.

His long black hair is braided.
He carries saddle blankets, rope and reins,
and in a monotone chants
strange words and names
of what it is he seeks.

I'd Like To Travel Like William Stafford

I'd like to travel like William Stafford
with one change of clothes
no matter how long the road,
a corner of the sky enough
as it was for William Stafford.

I'd like to see Sandhill cranes,
those great birds, his "lonely spears,"
pierce Oregon's ploughed fields.
If only a drought could be enough,
storm clouds escaping with their shadows.

But I'm weighted down with pots and pans,
trembling piles of read and unread books,
a closet piled with leather and cashmere.
Consumer, collector, nail biter, I unravel like yarn.
I'm nothing more than a shred of cirrus.

Old man Stafford, when he didn't travel light,
stood solid, planted as a northwest pine,
never uprooted by shiny gold and silver trinkets,
glad enough just to stand in a clearing,
pocketed hands, breathe beneath the stars,

as words space traveled toward him,
the light years of his morning hours,
traveled through fog thick with the music
of birds nested in his wild, green hair,
 flexing untried wings.

Points of Destination

1.
This is how I am absent in Rome
at rush hour, when a smart *Romana*,
stiletto boot fast to the pedal of her Vespa,
nearly razes me to the ground
in the Via Condotti
where I stand, map in hand,
dazed by the Spanish Steps in front of me,
resplendence circling me
like an adversary,
and I,
with no part to play,
nearly reduced to a ruin.

2.
I climb the winding road
no wider than a Peugeot
in the medieval hill town Castelnou,
shuttered this October evening
after the hot southern French summer,
shuttered against the cold and violence
of the Tramontane.
Here in the Pyrenees
in this emptied town,
flowers wilted, musicians
packed up, gone,
tiny wood doors,
lace-curtained windows, bolted,
I could be no one nowhere.

3.
In the Grand Café of Collioure
my red, metal chair feels vacant.
My pale, French waiter, looking bored
in the middle of his life,
avoids my glance,
folds and unfolds a serviette
over his greasy, black jacketed arm.
This is the season
abandoned by tourists.
I will never make the journey
to Nimes or Narbonne or Carcasonne,
places beyond those blue hills
without names I know.

4.
Suddenly I hate travel.
Hate it the moment the truth
exposes itself
in the beauty around me,
how it all simply goes on,
every gorgeous tiresome city,
every stately square,
cafés, palaces and playgrounds,
crowds of unknown faces
rushing to places I've never heard of
or seen or imagined —
all without me, nothing to do with me.
It is as if I were never
in the world at all,
or had already left it.
This is how I am absent.

Georgia and Sonya in Cambria, 2015.

Photo by Sonya Sabanac

Lois P. Jones

Self Portrait

they say the right eye is the eye
of the father
it hides beneath a mantle
of low clouds
only the left asks if we see its seeing
do we sense what aquafies
even as the photograph closes
in on itself everything around it
turned to black and white
the chiaroscuro it lives in
oceanic iris encircling
the pupil's isla negra
and its intake of breath
it is already forgetting
who it was
it is catching the last coin
of light as the dove coos
into the evening
something like a prayer

Red Horse

No one understood this blood run
to the moon, this blaze

of you, red horse in a swollen sky.
How you turned loose

like a fistful of fire ants.
How your temper could burn

a field when there was too much
to drink. There were days we'd spread

the blanket on the grasses
near the sycamores and let the desert

air run through us,
let the sage burn our nostrils

as we sipped a silky rioja.
A wine you liked to translate,

as you decoded everything beautiful.
Your lips full and slightly curled

siempre, siempre: jardin de mi agonia,
tu cuerpo fugitivo para siempre,

always, always: garden of my last breath,
your body escaped forever,

Lorca in his red shoes
lighting our tongues, lifting

our hips until the sun
turned poppy and burst.

Photo by Lois P. Jones

One

One lifetime she drank water from his skull.
She gilded the bones with gold and struck them
in the dirt. She pounced a vowel that was her name.
But now she is no one. She has the privilege
of ambiguity. Being one white woman,
being from nowhere but earth
and a father who lost his mind
in the metal.

Being this way, she is. An American,
indistinguishable as a flesh tree
in the desert. She wishes for a name
like Kandinsky, Levertov. How about Stradivarius?
How about dinner on the 41st floor? She did arrange this.
She did write the composer a letter.

Meet me on the roof of One Wilshire.

She brought wine and a white summer
dress. She brought nothing underneath them
but the long boulevard of empty offices
lit up like an afterthought. The cot
she carried up 11 flights of stairs. She brought
the night, slippery as a man on wheels.
She wheeled the stars until they were all
in their right places. She gave him all
the words an evening has for loneliness.

Shema!

Listen!, the Rabbi says, *God is One. Listen for what comes next.*
When death arrives shema is a mezuzah on the threshold
of your lives, the soul's last words before leaving a body.
But I no longer hear the hawk's cry above the city
where you left us. I can no longer count all the bones
that have buried themselves in me. Only the rabbi's voice,
this stranger who entered the last ten minutes of a life
when the daughters and all their hours could not give the word
to let you go. A woman who spoke past tubes and sheets,
beyond a face swollen from the fall and the eyelids sealed
past opening. She told you what a good job you'd done,
forgave all the secrets — the locked drawers finally open
their invisible contents drifting into the clinical air. Her words,
the blood moving through us as we held hands the road
and the river as we felt you pass, not so heavy as a song,
not even snow on the bough melting. I listened, I watched.
You were so silent, Mother, I could not hear you leave.

Günther's Tree

Because you are strong.
Because your branches span out ahead of you

and in so many years, age has allowed breadth to match height,
boughs so heavy with time they touch the ground.

Because a crow can land as easily as the butterfly
and a bench so perfectly placed beneath you

is shelter from the heat. Because all I want is to sleep
under your canopy, to dream of families that feasted

on acorns, cooked quail and rabbit on soft ground
near your roots. Because you sit among the dozens

of fragrant roses and the white arbor overlooking
an English garden — amid the bee palm and hibiscus

with its orderly wildness. I cannot distinguish water
that rushes over the fountain's stones from the wind

in your leaves. And this is music. And there is a shelter
like Mahler's little hut where the occasional deer can wander,

curious.

Oak tree at Descanso Gardens, Photo by Lois P. Jones

Trélex

I want windows to tell me their secrets
        so I don't have to see everything
                myself.

I want to know what the winter gave when it settled in,
a goose for nesting,
        a white crow
        on the bare cedar.

        How many
have flashed by — starlings around the steeple
        or swooped like the barn owl

        with wings only the dead can hear.

Who did the window watch all day in the pine grove
        until the cows were cutouts
                and the night went black with crows.

Which one bent their head down and into the frame —
        chose stubble fields   for a lost father.

How a photographer could strip the land

        of everything   but the leaving.

Which throat ate the flame anyway
        drank the wine until the bottles chattered
        their glass teeth.

        Whose hands knit the orange web
                then strung it from tree to tree
        spending yarn on a cool wind.

Who composed the song of the pear then hung it

from your note tree
> to flutter   at the slightest breath.

And when the wind flung the shutters open

> who cried with joy
> hearing the cows

and their chorus of wind chimes
> ringing, ringing, the night.

Photo by Lois P. Jones

The Scent of Ariel

When the shuttle arrives at the old wooden doors,
her luggage bulging with too many dresses
and *gringa* lotions, books she won't have time to open,
when the teenage boy smiles after hauling the world
four flights of terra cotta steps to her room
with views of Calle Canal and red rooftops
clinging to early winter warmth, it won't be
the earthy scent of pink geraniums outside her window
or last night's wood smoke and kerosene
that fills her lungs, but the freshly washed shirt
of the boy, neat as his perfect teeth, the scent —
part lather, part lavender. She won't call it innocence,
though it comes close. Closer is the lack of artifice,
the way she tries to lose her paleness by slipping
into a red *robozo*, the comfort of towels laundered
in sunshine. And if this country is not hers,
if some resent her place here, still Ariana
remembers her each year and brings extra towels
that smell sweet as a tamale husk, rough as a night
of too many sangrias when bells
of the Parroquia jangle like cast iron pans,
and she believes every tourist is a burro
without a master, grazing on what it can,
pretending there is somewhere to belong.

Winner of the Tiferet Poetry Prize

Foal

~ after reading "Fugue for Other Hands" by Joseph Fasano

In your next life you will be
birthed in needles
of hoarfrost, your eyes still
in the blue gauze between

this world and the next
and I will kneel so close
you will smell the hot iron
waiting to singe

your skin. You'll hear
the crackle of the flame
and your throat will prickle
with stars. I'll wrap your shins

in nettle and this shelter will fall
deeply into zero. This is the start
of your suffering for the children,
yours who became

the wanderers, beaten between
the withers, broken and unridable
in the world's dark loam. There is
no animal to save you now

no purling stream to fold
shame into, not even the jackdaw
as witness, or a single crofter
awake in this cat's eye hour.

Revenge tries on its black
bridle then drapes it over
the swinging fence.
Father, I will not take out

your eyes but I will brand you
with the word you fear
and you will wear it
and you will wear it

and give up everything to winter.

The Landscape of Flight

> ~ *for Susan R.*
> *Once you have tasted flight you will walk the earth with*
> *your eyes turned skywards,*
> *for there you have been and there you will long to return.*
> ~ *Leonardo da Vinci*

1. Bone

They say a hawk landed in your cradle
and swept its tail feathers past your mouth,
awakening a taste for flight,
your need to pull the buzzard apart
with slender fingers looking for secrets
in articulated wings. Here
in the late hours, the scent of wax burns
your nostrils as you pry the codex,
cracking the contours, drawing
the downy tufts in two. You note
the breast bone shaped like a keel,
lay out each pearled shaft
until it reclaims its shape. Candles come
and go like sylphs, casting shadows
on the freshly inked sketches. When you finally
walk the corridor to your room,
feathers fall to the tiled floors, lodge
in your velvet robes and pillows.

Sleep arrives
       slender as a wing bone.   You dream you are
a black crane flying low across the Arno,
               the moon a plume nearly gone.

2. *Earth*

I've been trying for so long
to leave you, but gravity
pulls me back.
Maybe my wings
are too solid,
my breath heavy as salt,
bones too dense for the folds
of space where nothing
answers my call.

3. *Flower*

Look at these dogwood blossoms
caught in the act of flying,
white wings bent and touching
in a flock of origami.
They could be cranes adrift
       in the impermanence of dying.

Kousa Dogwood Blossoms by Peter Shefler

Susan Rogers

Essay

I believe that successful art of any genre whether it be poetry or painting, music or dance lifts our hearts and spirits creating a bridge between our third dimensional physical world and the unseen spiritual world which governs it. It is also a bridge that can connect and integrate the different aspects of ourselves, our physical self, our emotional self and our spiritual self. We experience works of art with our senses, we receive positive energy from them and they engage and stimulate our emotions and our intellect. And if the art resonates deeply with us it can change us at a deep soul level. Art can help us to become brighter, more joyful and it can shift us in our core so that we vibrate at a higher frequency and come closer to our true, divine nature.

In that sense, creating art can be an act of giving to others, a form of service and prayer. Moreover, experiencing those works of art deeply in ways which elevate our spirit and bring us an appreciation of beauty and a greater sense of awareness of who we are and why we are here can be considered an aspect of spiritual health.

After I became a practitioner of Sukyo Mahikari, I felt not only empowered by words but enlightened by them. Great poetry was not only a combination of music and truth but it carried light. It was a bridge of light. I learned that words carry power and divinity within them and that they possess *kototama*, the spiritual essence of their sounds. I also understood that words have the capacity to inspire and guide people into a greater awareness of their own sacred nature and their responsibility to nurture that higher aspect of themselves. The Sukyo Mahikari teachings gave me a sense of my own purpose in writing and a direction for my life. Also, after I was introduced to the teachings of Sukyo Mahikari and to the great masters who transmitted these teachings I felt a newfound sense of confidence and authority in my writing. I was connected through the teachings and these great teachers to a lineage of light that was peerless and that held a wealth of wonder. I perceived poetry as a tool to mine that wealth and to lift the vibration of my soul and others to a higher plane.

I am encouraged in this endeavor by Kotama Okada's vision of the coming spiritual civilization which promises to include the arts. I feel great happiness knowing there will be a place for the arts in the bright, spirit-centered future. I also feel that I have been given an identity as a spiritual poet or a poet of light, who walks hand in hand with our sacred source to help bring about a high-dimensional, spirit-first world.

The Westside Women Writers (WWW) is a group of poets that offers me support in fulfilling that mission as a poet of light and as a bridge of connection. When I joined WWW, I felt that I had not merely joined a community of like-minded poets, but that I had entered a diverse group that represented a wealth of different experience and a wide range of poetic styles and voices. I am grateful to each of these gifted poets for sharing their voices and inspiration, for blessing me with their insight, generosity of spirit and kind-hearted critique and for our workshops which have allowed me to polish my poetry so it can shine.

~ **Susan Rogers**

The Origin is One

~ *for Kotama Okada*

The dove knows the way
follow her.

Your heart knows the way
listen well.

Within your deepest self
are wings of light.

They cover the earth
with waves of love.

Do you remember?
You once knew.

Stand in the warmth
of sunlight and recall.

The origin of the world
is one.

The origin of religions
is one.

The origin of all
humankind is one.

Circle back.
Imagine the great will

of all things
stirring in your fingers.

Reach out your arms
and open your palms

to the sky.
It is time.

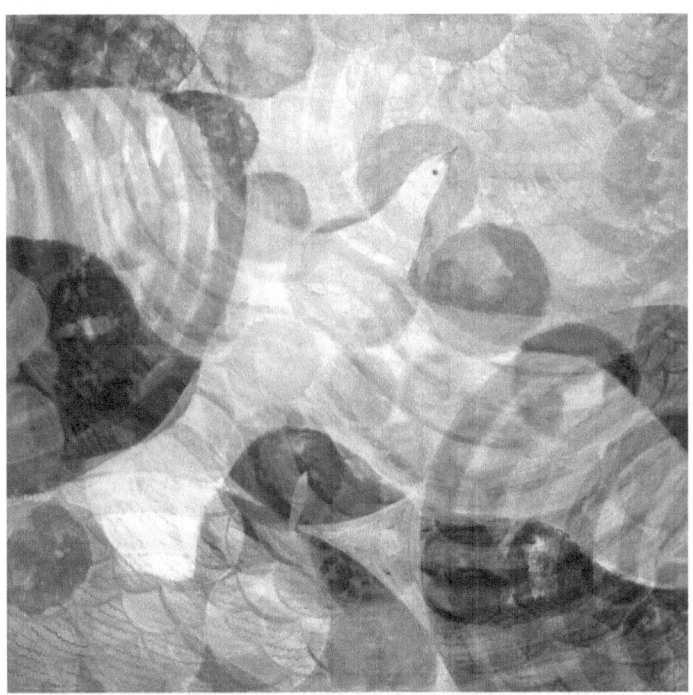

"Searching" by Susan Dobay.

Kuan Yin

~ *for Keishu Okada*

Kuan Yin by Susan Rogers

You sit upon a pedestal of jade
milk green, your light flows liquid from within,
pulsing prayer through rivulets of stone.
And so you are a contradiction, made
hard jade, yet soft like sacred love, Kuan Yin.
You guide me even now. Through you I own
my stiff resistance to God's grace. Afraid
to melt, I keep my edges hard and in
my heart I keep your love, for me alone.
Your right eye holds a tear forever laid
in stone; it holds me too. I drink you in,
search for your source of peace, the deep calm known
and shared by you. Within the jade, Kuan Yin
it's here. I remember now — compassion.

Grass
~ *for Koo Okada and Amritanandamayi*

Yesterday, someone I know
looked through me like I wasn't there
as if I were a field of air,
insubstantial and invisible.
Today, I think of my great teacher who said,
"Become a practitioner of humility,"
and a modern saint who said,
"A cyclone can destroy the mightiest of trees,
but even a cyclone cannot touch the grass.
This is the greatness of humility."
So today I have decided to become like grass
which needs no encouragement
but water, sun, sky,
which is invisible, often, as we walk by.
It is true the grass is sometimes mowed,
but that just keeps it safe from storms,
close to the ground, close to you.
Oh, God of all things great and small,
cyclone, trees, dirt,
let me strive to always be like grass,
cool comfort for the earth,
so that children may run through me
barefoot on a summer day,
and I may greet them, or catch them if they fall,
soft and green and sweet, with no resistance
to their play, almost invisible —
pure reason for their joy.

First Night in Takayama

On the occasion of the 50th Anniversary Ceremony of Light, Takayama, Japan

~ after Lois P. Jones' "Last Night in Barcelona"

If ever a woman could be born
in a moment like a dragon cloud
appearing at sunset
large as a golden God
curving over the mountains
sunlit form and reddening sky
startling the silent passengers
on a Takayama bound bus
with unfathomable presence —
a chance meeting of light
and burnished gold
looming at the very entrance
to the city of the High Mountain
with its tremor of echoing bells,
it is tonight.

This evening of cool, clear air
fills your chest with breath completely,
inhale washing through
like pure spring water
just like the air you welcomed
at the train station in Atami,
where the very air entered
as liquid light
and every cell drank.

Tonight,
in the pause between
gold and deepening blue,

between the first stage of things
and the next,
you can almost hear
the symphony beginning.

It is now the time
you have been waiting for.
It is now the point
where the great wave curves
back upon itself, rising
in a leftward spiral towards light.
The Golden Dragon Koryu
guides you from the sky,
hovering like a living cloud
in a sea of pure love,
sweeping over you and everyone
on the bus with a flourish

of anticipation, with a greeting
that says, "Welcome.
You have come."
It lifts you
into the city of your highest self,
raising each thread
of your intricate, woven being
into a higher spin,
until every part of you sings.
As you align with the new wave,
you ride into Takayama
on a crest of gratitude,
in a chorus of harmony,
into the spirit first world,
into the era of wonder,
your heart's new dance.

Longing for October

Photo by Susan Rogers

I looked for you
among leaves
so full of color

they burst
like cherry flames
singing of sap.

I looked for you
in the blood of autumn—
trees warmed by sunfire,

spinning in the pulse
of maple and beech
anthocyanin sugaring

green veins
as spring sugars
the sky with sakura.

I looked for you
in the chill of autumn,
mountains filling

the sweep of space
with strokes of brilliance
knowing it is both

fire and frost
that paints the tree,
knowing every love

turns to deeper shades
of longing as it rises
into fullness.

You are wind
and water moving
across the face of leaves.

You are the invisible
made visible,
sap rising

until it explodes
in a symphony of light,
everywhere I look

in the canopy.

What the Trees Say

~ from Toyama, Japan

In the shrine
of an unknown God
I follow the path
of seekers.

We have come
to this holy ground
charged with light
to offer respect and prayer.

The tour leader
does not know whom
is honored here
or how to address

our greeting properly.
He knows the language
of the country but cannot
decipher the name of God

from the weathered sign
at the entrance to the shrine.
I am at a loss as how to pray
or speak in harmony

with this ancient place.
So many Gods
which one is here?

I pause at the top
of many steps
admiring light
sifting through leaves,
bringing every color

into clarity.
Where are the answers
that I need? I wrap
my arms around a tree

and lean there,
listening.
In quiet, I hear,
"Love."

The second one
says, "Focus."
The third is silent.
As is the fourth,

but I wait there
measuring silence,
sinking into the heart
of tree,

until I finally hear,
"Hope,"
the warmth
of an inner knowing

filling me,
these unknown trees —
this light filled sky
and I in communion.

Across Bridges

~ for Lois P. Jones

How the flicker of a smile
crosses from one to another,
the opening of a heart

in gentle motion
like the first flutter
of a butterfly wing

testing the morning light.
Where are our gentle wings?
How easy to fly

across bridges
of unfolding
like quick wind

unknowingly.
Yet the woman
on her way to work

is here, and you are here
and I am here in your smile
that crosses Sky Bridge —

in your memory of coffee
and the putting on of shoes.
Sometimes I want to open

into your day,
walk inside,
the gentle lifting,

thoughtful wondering
that emerges from the presence
of another heart.

We cross every day
so easily, yet without meeting.
The flower in front of me

quivers and the butterfly
above it sails. I had almost forgotten
to say, "Good morning."

Photo by Lois P. Jones

Shiawase

White butterfly,
air dancer,
sudden sunlight
caught in a breath.

I ask you to land
on my hand.
Oh irrepressible light —
shiawase.

I cannot command
nor anticipate your flight.
Only reach out
to you

near the fluttering flower,
planter of fragrant herbs,
tomato vine,
without expectation.

Quiet my heart
as you circle
the colors I have planted,
blessing them.

Shiawase: Japanese word for happiness

The Poem Inside

The poem
inside the orange
peals its bright

tang into my mouth
of awareness
singing full

sweet sensation
into the juice
of every section

of me, coursing
sunfire and
music into

every vein,
every seed,
filling the pulp

of empty,
unengaged space
with intention,

with the alchemy
of creation,
the momentary

verve
of pure vibration.
The poem inside

the orange
is written
in the orange

before I can hold
the orange
in my hand,

or taste its
flash of light
upon my tongue—

before the orange
even becomes
orange.

It sounds
deeply in that place
where all sound

originates,
pealing
away the rind

of things
into their essential
pattern, pealing

into bells and bells
of recombinant song
that flood

our universe
with harmony,
poetry,

waves
upon waves
of being.

And the Soul Shall Dance

And the heart shall sing
and the eyes shall open
into the bright purple,
into the melting pink
of a new dawn,
of a realm bathed
in a wash of love,
in the rhythm of quiet,
where boundaries blur,
where sky and mountain marry.
At the edge of the clear river,
at the base of the flowering tree,
there is a country of compassion,
there is a welcome invitation.
Here, even leaves are spirit.
Here, even birds are joy.
No need for shoes,
no need for memory.
Come as you are;
come as you wish to be.
Bring your music;
bring your knowing —
Only gratitude and humility,
only unity of your heart's desire
with what is simply blessed and given
with what is born of ancient fire
dances in this peaceful glen —
dances in a round, again and again.
Higher and higher, your soul shall dance —
higher and higher.

This Lotus

Photo by Susan Rogers

To awake,
to dream,
to open again
into first light,
awash with gold.
Each and every petal
kissed with the sun's love,
kissed with the memory of mud,
blessed with the touch of water.
Opening and opening,
again and again,
lifetime after lifetime,
pond after pond,
poem after poem,
until it is beyond
dream, water, mud,
beyond the innocence
of first light, beyond
even the kiss of sun —
there, where it is all
written.

What Returns

~ after Rilke's "What Survives"

I say nothing vanishes
or is entirely beyond reach
even the flight of a phoenix
or the sound of petals
in a garden where all petals

have gone. You carry
the glint of gold
even after I
have lost trace of it.
I remember fire after you.

Sonya Sabanac

Poetry – Everlasting Moments

Poetry is the world of its own; it a magical place where one could find his own feelings and experience in other people's memories. As photography, Poetry captures moments that will forever speak to readers from different time and places and will not necessarily tell the same story. For me, Poetry is also a time-machine. It allows me to travel back and forth, from past into present and even go to future. I can freeze time at any moment I like, thus preventing certain things from happening. Poetry savors the moments of life; sometimes the painful ones, sometimes happy or just every-day, ordinary ones. Being an immigrant, not by a choice, but rather by circumstances beyond my control, it is important for me to re-visit my past and find a way to store what was vitally important. Perhaps I am re-building my lost home from memories; a place that cannot be taken away from me.

Poetry is a blessing, it does heal, whether one writes or read. Reading other people's poetry is like stepping into a different kind of realm. It has multiple benefits. First of all, finding one's own thoughts and sentiments in other's people's work is uplifting. If one was lonely, after reading poetry would be less so or not at all. For the people who mourn the loss of the loved one, Poetry could be a great comfort. Furthermore, the poems are offering so many different worlds. Books do take us on a journey. Poets have an extra pair of eyes so they see what an ordinary person cannot. Poets are also missionaries. They are saving the world. I imagine Poetry being a river that runs across the most beautiful places; we just need to let that river take us to wherever it's running.

Mayakovski said in one of his poems "How to stick a tender word into a thick ear?" I would say that no one has such a thick skin that gentle words cannot get under.

Poetry awakes humanity in every each of us. For me Poetry is a sunny island in the midst of the Cold Ocean. Some are afraid that poetry may lose readers, but I am convinced that Poetry as our spiritual daily bread will never lessen its importance in life.

Being a member of WWW Poetry Group gives me a comfort, hope and inspiration. I am very grateful to each of my friends for giving me a piece of their mind, for inspiring me to write and explore. I admire their dedication and mission. This comradeship brings humility and sense of uniqueness at the same time.

~ **Sonya Sabanac**

A Magical Prayer

Perhaps there is a prayer that resolves and pardons everything
and I could, unknowingly,
utter it one night
and wake up in the morning
to find out that I am quite content
in this new reality.
That truth is sitting comfortable in me
molding a new person
out of a thousand old clashes.
And I would stop
and look back into the eyes of the wolf
I was running away from,
but I would only see a stray dog.

For whatever happens in your life,
there is a prayer that resolves
and pardons everything,
but no words are needed.
This magical prayer is spoken
simply by
         accepting.

NOTE: *The first line is taken from a poem "In a Circle"*
       by Miroslav- Mika Antic

No Man's Land

The younger people did not see any signs.
The older were saying all along there would be war,
the signs were everywhere:
a wagon of money could buy so little,
the lice appeared out of nowhere and spread like wildfire,
the women giving births to sons
to make up for the men that would vanish;
the fruit-trees so fertile, their branches touching the ground
under the weight of fruits
as if someone whispered to their roots this was last
to bear life before death comes.

* * *

Early morning, while their beds
were still warm
one man, a child and a woman
hastily left their home. They locked
the door — an ordinary thing to do
as if going for a walk,
as if there was no war
as if they would soon be back home.

Running to save their lives,
they did not know they were running
away from them. They will never be the same,
this was a moment of irreversible change.
Shall we stop them while they are still standing
in front of the door and shout: "Wait,
wait and re-think if you really want to go."

But they would not hear,
the distance of time would muffle our voices.

The girl carries her school back-pack
with a big clock on it.
Many times they all laughed
watching the cat stalk the second hand,
she would measure the distance
and then jump to catch her prey,
but it was only a game.

In April of 1992 in Sarajevo — nothing was a game.
Death screamed from the sky,
even the birds were in disarray.
In the empty space between two forced
borders within the same city,
like a glacier, heavy and cold,
a silence lay and deep in it,
with vultures eyes the snipers lurked.

It is too late to turn back.
The three stepped into danger
like featherless birds out in the open.
"Be casual, do not run, show no fear,
walk straight, the other side is only
30 meters away."
Were the snipers measuring their steps
deciding at what particular place
of this no man's land
they would stop their walk?
And who would go first?
Whose blood would satisfy them most?

Their feet are heavy, it feels as if
they were walking on the mine's field.
What if those hidden hands
are playing Russian Roulette?
The woman's hand sweats holding
her daughter's hand.

Who or what saved them that April morning?
Was it a girl's pale face or a new life
in the woman's womb?

They crossed from the "East" to the "West"
and further away they went.
The woman gave birth to a son
whose sole reason to come was to save
his family. Having fulfilled his mission,
he rested on the earth for 36 hours
and then returned to the unknown
place he came from.
The man, the girl and the woman never
came back to unlock their home.

Mirjana

~ *Volim te Mama Moja*

"I was born old" she used to say,
not bitter but with a smile.
Skipped teenage foolishness
and vanity of womanhood,
No red lipstick, no high heels,
no fashionable dresses.
When her daughter would suggest
to dye her hair, she would waive
a hand as if she was driving a fly away.

But she loved to host!

Everyone was welcome to her home,
neighbors and family,
friends and people she spent few hours with in the train,
a beggar that rang at her door.
Everyone was welcome!
She would sit her guests
at the dining table
and feed them with the best meals she cooked:
a chicken soup and roasted pork, red potatoes,
béchamel and tomato sauce, cabbage salad,
cheese crapes and what not!
She would serve the best brandy made
from her Slavonia's sweet plums
and then they would talk

and the laugh would rush out of her throat.
And when she was laughing,
her whole body was shaking;
her laughter would lift the room.

"I was born old" she used to say,
not bitter,
but with a smile of the one
who came to the place of wisdom
before the rest of us.

Kristina Hugging The Tree

Her face glows
and her eyes are closed
as she inhales the scent of pine.
This is her tree of life.
It is green and not yet tall,
but the sky offers so much space to grow.

She knows some trees
are cut short —
some by lighting
some by violent hands,
some simply dry out
at the peak of their lives
and only God knows numbers
of branches and leaves that
will blossom on each tree.

Kristina's tree was shaken
by the gusty winds
and she reached out to The Only Hand
that could walk her through the storm.

She survived the opacity of hospital days,
long hours with syringes in her veins but
she is hugging a tree now
and her face glows. She is in bliss,
each moment
is a treasured gift.

Kristina. Photo by Sonya Sabanac

Somewhere Far Across the Ocean

The siren screams into
a wet
cold morning.
The ship is leaving.
At the dock mainly women
wrapped in woven scarfs
their faces full of fears and tears.
Watching them from the deck
wounded women become one.
Why am
I
leaving?
My vision turns blurry.
The shoreline is disappearing
and we are too into a mist and fog.
Water is angrily rolling underneath.

Waking up two centuries later,
the same scream
stabs my heart like a dagger,
only this time it's a train siren.
Still dark outside.
Perhaps,
in my dreams
I was someplace else,
where roots of trees
spread deep into a ground.

Listening to what my heart
beat is trying to tell me,
I am seeking the truth,
justification,
perhaps seeking a pardon.

Am I ever going to find home?

Photo by Sonya Sabanac

Shifting Balance

In the year my mother died,
my daughter sent me a photo from Morocco.
Behind the secretive,
terracotta street of Marrakesh,
my daughter looks straight into the camera
neither sad nor smiling,
her arms crossed in the calm of acceptance
and for the first time I see not a child
but a woman.

Then I turned to the mirror,
a woman grown older
looks back,
new lines gave harshness to her face
as if sadness erased the hope.

My mother disappeared into the blue
and I have become her
and my daughter me,
but with this shifting a hope was born
that our own holy trinity would be restored.
For, from another end of that blue
a child may come
and I will await with all the lullabies
ready to open my arms.

The Last Call

I was a wanderer last night
and came across a Garden of my Childhood.
A magical place where possible and impossible
things were happing at equal rate.

Our little soldiers standing all around, ready
to guard our missions,
tents made hastily before the rain,
ships on which we sailed
over the ocean,
the bicycles lined up for the next grand slam race.

During the winter,
as our yard would turn into the white
vastness, we would reach the Northern Pole
and make igloos even Eskimos would approve of.
But it was the spring that would truly unleash us.
In the rhythm of the Bonanza theme
we would ride horses for hours,
chasing those "wanted dead or alive."

As days grew longer, swelled with heat
and linden scent,
it was time to be daring, time to test
our strength and survival skills.
We would pack up our caravans
and dress as Bedouins,
cross the Sahara in straight three-hour walk.

Some other times, we wanted an adventure

extraordinaire, to go far and beyond what eye can see
"The Journey into the Center of the Earth"
was a perfect fit.

Mysterious, dark and mossy
hollowness of the old mulberry tree
was where we started this trip.

And there were times
when we did not want to go
anywhere. Instead, we stayed in
our city where we had important roles:
doctors, teachers, pilots, nurses and
everything else our city needed us to be.

We lived in peace
until the boys had enough
and declared war. Then, a new game was on.

Slowly, our day would come to its end.
From the lighted windows,
our mothers would call us home.
As one, we would say
"I want to play more."
And they would let us,
once, twice.
When the day-light dimmed out
there was a last call
to which we did not dare say "no."

Decades passed by
and we still like to play,

still search for that perfect role.
One by one,
our mothers gone
but still looking after us
from their windows above.
When all that is left of our day
is just a night,
they would call us again,
"Children, it is time
to come home."

Photo by Sonya Sabanac

The South Tower

~ *for Diana*

The cab drives through the streets of Beverly Hills.
I see beautiful houses and inviting green gardens
but my heart will not stop the tremor,
cannot convince me that this season of Spring
will renew us, as it renews the Earth.

Arriving at destination,
for a moment longer I observe the world.
The big city noise and everything in motion.

I enter the South Tower — Silence.
This is a parallel world of unknown origin.
Passing the nurse station,
a ghost of my crushed hopes jumps at me;
I am not new to this, but with each visit
my legs are shorter.
What will I learn? My body perspires.

My innocent friend is lying on the pillows.
She was always content like a baby,
as if she was living in a perfect world,
a good wisher, all made of kindness,
her face is now like petals of a white rose
her dark eyes — ponds of sadness.
The air in the room is still, as if time stopped,
yet we both know it is rapidly running.

I take her hand in silence,
looking at some distant point, she says:
"I have a beautiful family,
they do not deserve this."

Upon Listening to the Sretensky Monastery Choir

Is it only thirty men
or does the entire universe sing?
They expand from barely a whisper
to the full, omnipresent voice
that pulls us deep in
and their music is a time machine,
so we travel back
and live the past:
Love, fate,
wars and death.

I am shaken to the root,
my Slavic Soul flies!

Embodied memories
not entirely all mine,
the pictures are passing through my mind
like singing solders coming home from the war.

A little girl is sitting on the grass
with a cloth doll in her lap.

Vecernji Zvon,
The Evening Bell!
The village is falling into silence;
The steppe so wide and white
fading light.

Inside the houses, with just a few branches,
mothers are keeping embers alive;
That harsh voice of poverty, inherited.

The young man is walking fast,
somewhere,
behind the last house
he will kiss his future bride,
"*Batjuska*, it is good to be alive!"
But when the wheat ripens,
the Cossacks would bring his body
on a horse-drawn cart.

Pain, fate, wars
dying a little with each loss.
How much sadness a heart can hold?
My Slavic Soul, where do you go?

The White Fields of Sky

Every day, like a soldier
my brain wakes up
into the same march.
For years fed with words
of no meaning or purpose,
it longs for the white fields of sky.

It's cracking. Rebelling at last!

And through those cracks,
my mind gets out.
First slowly, just peeking,
wary, as if afraid of darkness
to collide with.
Then it recognizes
the sounds it was once fully
consumed with.
Time is not a straight line
but a circle with many pockets.
From that single,
unexpected moment of recognition
everything comes to life.

This is love!

Not just any,
but the one that runs deep
like an underground river
that almost hurts plunging in.
The only valid fear
is the fear of not loving.

Kathi Stafford

Photo by Daniel Martin

Tulsa Town

Eighth grade meant only one thing at Edison Middle School in Tulsa: Mrs. Fast's poetry project. Everyone whispered in the halls about her torturous assignments, but this one was the most feared. We were supposed to come up with sonnets, haikus, villanelles—the list went on and on. I remember my mother carefully typing up each and every attempt for my lime green folder. One day while we were working on our project, Mrs. Fast played songs from a Joan Baez album on the turntable in her room. "Now THAT is poetry!" she thundered at us, waggling her black eyebrows rapidly as she spoke.

I was no Joan Baez, nor was I Emily Dickinson, floating mysteriously behind thin screens in white, flowing dresses. I wasn't even a Wallace Stevens, even though I've now practiced corporate law for many years. But I did manage to get an A+ on my poetry project, which is the only grade I remember from middle school. I felt hooked on the beauty of rhythm and beats and nuance and sounds and shaded memory, just like that.

In the USC professional writing program, majoring in poetry, I learned about different worlds from Syd Field, even though he taught us about screenwriting, and Janet Fitch, with her poetic fiction. I think a good poem tells a story, and the writer has to think about acts in sequence, as well as the drama of the plot. These fantastic teachers (and others) expanded their students' understanding of literature and art.

Millicent Borges Accardi set up the Westside writers poetry group about eight years ago, initially inviting people who had earned their masters from the USC program. The writing efforts were at a strong level, and the work has continued to strengthen through the years. The talk at our gatherings ranges from films to artists to spiritual journeys to our very different heritages. The brilliance of these writers is always so inspiring—and so humbling.

In closing, I encourage you to think about what inspires you in your daily life and how you are able to express your creativity. My son writes lyrical music and lovely poetry. My daughter plays violin and creates amazing handmade books. We each have our gifts, so explore yours and find out what feeds it—and what you are able to place in your own lime green folder. Right now, I am drawn to gardening (where strawberries and onions co-exist in peace), Puccini's operas, aimless walks at the airport park, white orchids, and Jesse Stone movies. Each of these activities lead me back to the writing page and the joy of creation.

~ **Kathi Stafford**

These Bones

—in the shadow of Bryce Canyon
The hieroglyphic code from these bones
Puts on a shadow play. Ulna turns to dust
Within my body. When will the crest of pain
Die down, recede on the pebbled edge
Of the tributary?
Oh my bones. How I took you for granted,
Never bearing my full weight in the whirl
Along the banks of the Paria River. I pray
Mercy for cartilage   sinew   nerves

Photo by Sonya Sabanac

Division

We used to hold
hands near the bower. Now, we lean together,
quiet, and that is enough.

Evening came fast—too dark to look
for avocados any more. The sprawling
tree filled the yard, its branches large
and smoky brown. A tangy scent
floats at dusk as honeysuckle
clusters atop the wooden fence
and hangs above the hedges.

Perhaps my cells split
sideways as I sat on the bench
in the silence. I asked him to pick the
fruit, but the hour was late. A woman light
on her path keeps moving anyway.

Hive

A tablespoon of honey and Aunt Lolly makes me
Swallow the comb   my throat
Tickles   tiny wings scrape me close
Spit out the wax when she's not looking
My little bee might miss his sisters   or not
Let's call him Fred for now
Next day Aunt Ruth steers the station wagon
Halfway across the state   encased in teak
Over to Glass Mountains   though they're barely a
Mesa but we don't argue   My tiniest toe
Hurts but I keep still
Auntie glows on the crest   transformation
We scoot down the hill   on our butts all the way
Dodging bees but looking for Fred   My cousins and
I build an altar for worship   near Rattlesnake Lake
Stone on stone meant for fire   Oklahoma
Plains   spread out   every which way   in a
Season of tall grass and barley rustling in the vicious
Wind where I am simply myself   a small girl in a big prairie

Blank Check

One year ago today: my first go
at radiation. The tech with his arms
full of blue tattoos and scars eases me
into place. The quiet clicking

Machine drones on as I hold still
in its shadow. A thin red light razors
below my skin, down into an ocean
of cells and fear. In a few weeks, my skin will

Come off—each strip delicate
and lacy. So individual, each layer
with its sheer story of my past. Some women
are stronger than I am.

Thirty-three times I go home after and fall
into sleep, so hard and final.

I win the lottery. One year come
and gone
with no new lumps. This is a gift
and a wonder to me. Will there always be
a blank check made out
to future scars?

Maybe I never ask the right questions.
There's a tale for every traveler.

The tech guy talks on about his newborn,
Jimmy, three months old, while he shines
with joy. He's trying to distract me. I know.

I lie still and
take it all in.

My pain held up on all four corners
by the prayers lifted by my saints, my friends, towards
gentle sky, oh Metta, oh peace of my soul.

Photo by Kathi Stafford

To May in her coma after the motorcycle

Those three sisters keep telling you to *go on*,
We'll be fine, just let go. Natasha, her sweater
Tight as always, leans over you with her sharp
Teeth gleaming. Your wreck of a family, you
Used to joke. I say, *Stay, stay, spit death in the eye,*

Arm wrestle, kick him when he's down. Those
Girls have calculators in their back pockets, to punch
Out their cut of that house in the Hollywood
Hills. Oh how you ricocheted across my night sky
That time we stayed up in a forest 'til three and talked Kafka.

Don't write me in your lines, you'd whisper,
All annoyed but still hoping I would. And
That time you said, *You don't have to wait for the pain*
To end to be happy. The smartest girl, that was you,
May, named for your Da's old girlfriend, not the story

To bring up around Ma. Oh, you so tough and
Relentless, street lights at the county museum crashing on your
Rosy smile while you kicked my first guy in the shins. Now
blood not pulled
By tides — it's all machinery now, gridlocked around your sacred
bed. I sneak in
After hours, burn sage in the corners, hiss against silence.

Desire

I thought I could write a song about
that painting. Desire. That's all the paint
told me, spelled it out in
cursive, purple and buttery.

Did he tell the neighbors about the apples.
Someone wants food, sex,
poetry. The weekend after Saturday brunch.
You eat then you go to bed.

The tall blondes gossip in the corner. The
room full of art vibrates around them, levitates
slightly. Their eyes close
in unison.

Photo by Sonya Sabanac

Never Unlock

I would never unlock the door for Tommy,
even though he was first chair in the trumpets —
always smoking on breaks, even after the conductor
warned him about Marlboros and their toll.

Every Thursday he'd show up at our old blue house
on Fifth and Pine, humming Sousa outside my window.
One week he'd tap lightly, other days he'd beat
that door like it was the bass drum. He stole reeds

from the oboes even though he couldn't use them,
just to piss off those three smart girls
with their glares. I still wore braids even though
I was too old for them. Tommy felt like a hornet's nest,

bleak and layered, his camel coat smelling of polish
and old cigars. He'd tell bad jokes and make the brass
section roar until Mr. Scizzor would send him
to the principal's office. Tommy made fun of us

violins and violas, called us wusses,
but stared at us anyway. My bow would waver
under his eye and I'd mess up all those crazy sixteenths
from Mozart , botch up every run.

How could I have unlocked that door? We
would have pulled out my shiny violin, he'd
have yowled on his trumpet. That music
heat would have clouded up every clear

high note I still held back. Instead, I shone through
the peep hole each week, stopped breathing,
watched Tommy spinning his case
in his scarred and starry hands.

Photo by Maja Trochimczyk

Ambika Talwar

Poetry of Source Within

Ethics, too, are nothing but reverence for life...
~ Albert Schweitzer, Civilization and Ethics, 1949

"*The Sanskrit root matr-, to measure, is the source of the word for matter itself, as well as material, matrix, metre and maya - the Indian concept of the illusion of measuring and dividing that we live by, and from which we must eventually free ourselves.*"
http://fusionanomaly.net/sanskrit.html

In the beginning is Desire, self-creating Intelligence.

In the expansive-expanding golden matrix of our consciousness, we are self-sustaining, self-evolving, and self-restricting act of "*poesis*" (creating) herself. Gaps arise in our knowing, willing, and doing. We plumb to duality, and shadows rise as warnings and teachings. Herein, too, stirs the many-splendored poetic, a tug between multitude shades of reality. Of course, we are seduced by negating forces, the push and pull of the universe within and without.

Isn't such a collision an impetus towards new creation?

We have been in such creation-destruction cycles for millions of years. Even though we continue to be errant in our ways, it is clear that the only way to understand our unities is to be aware of the poetic principle and awaken to something ineluctable, to the mystery. When we are thus aware, we recognize an inherent goodness in the weave. In such awareness, poetry (re-ordering the beauty of the world) becomes a moral act.

Poetry is an utterance (*shruti*), a call from our deepest memory (*smriti*).

Poetry reveals the grammar of origins, a language, which offers us a paradigm for our perceptual awareness. In our spiraling cycles is our co-evolution. Grammar resides in our bodies, our "wireless anatomy" (Dr. Randolph Stone) of whorls and spirals, that also contain the golden proportions. Since *meter*, *mater*, and measure have the same root, and our bodies are in harmony with nature and the kosmos, what we create must be imbued with such aesthetic; hence, affect of poetry is morality.

Many tales of creation powerfully proclaim the world's wonders and declare that we be guardians of its beauty. Indeed, Earth and kosmos are entrusted to us and we must be good caretakers. Poetry (from *poesis* to create/ing) is process and form that remind us of the Intelligent ordering of the cosmos and our continual relationship with it. The declaration, "*In the beginning was the word, and the word was made flesh*" itself proclaims our self-creating desire.

Could we not see such created energy fields as powered to generate and illumine universal laws? That such knowledge of our origins resides in our minutest energetic structures? And, very simply, when we discover the "breath inside the breath" (Kabir), may we not recreate our environs on immanent and transcendent principles of sentience? Shall we not be awakened, be fully alive?

Such a process of self-arising in unity itself is poetic. So life flourishes.

In summation, here is a paradigm.

* Poetry is a weave (reflection) of the self-arising intelligent dynamic principle.
* This weave (word given flesh) is an emergence towards wholeness — aesthetics and ethics in a natural flow of contraction and expansion. We swing between states of sleep and awakening urging shifts in relational fields of consciousness.
* The movement towards a new poetics (now a clarion call) enlivens beauty inherent in our matrix. In such light, we cannot *"be false to any wo-man"* (sic). Poetry must transform and heal us through our passion to revere sentience.
* Because life is sacred and interconnected, shall we not be guided by ethical principles of collaboration and cooperation?
* Will such poetic process guide our future, for poets are not only activists but also activators. As the world's *"unacknowledged legislators"* (P. B. Shelley), are we not responsible for our continuing unfoldment and stirring same in others?

As a narrative of our beginnings and the world's great mythic traditions, the *poeisis* process explores the forming and dissolution of cosmic elements and reflects the cyclic nature of being and non-being, darkness and silence; hence we have rhythm, which gives rise to meter. Our paradigms are universal. Scottish novelist John Buchan noted: "God gave us poetry out of His great compassion, not so our age can chatter to itself, but so that all ages may converse." Thus connected like universal god/desses, we must be inherently ethical, so remain in coherence with our universe, for kosmic rhythm is harmony.

Questions like: What is it that matters to you? Who are you? What makes you?" are not easy to answer. Answers may lie in poetry: a journey in self-recovery through self-reflection, the most self-reflexive art that is revelation!

She/Shakti is a journey to our inherent godhood: *That moving sculpture is god(dess)--a repository-container of all frequencies (known and unknown, measured and immeasurable) in a harmonized dynamic whole dancing in its perfect stillness--Self-reflexive and inter-active-being–Sexing the universe at will and at pleasure--in truth and gratitude–blissed in playfulness–Spawning universes at will–marking infinitudes–in resonant balance of breath and being–knowing both the dark and the light.*

Eating the Light

XXXIV.

A word, a mirror
sings of mysteries, of light

A child, I look into the water
see wild clouds
like horses' tails streaming
for the farthest apple
a fabric that wraps divinity

Water slowly trickles then drips
I extend my hand and collect the drops
and exult in its taste.

~ **Ambika Talwar**

Hunger of Fire-Flies

Hordes of fire-flies winking merge in your dark merlot
to hide fingers curling a happy goblet.
        How many moons peer at silent storm, a quiet parting!

Dancing moon with flute sidles by fireflies, hundreds
intent on play – too busy to care this blazing
        summer night… my skin sings in the silence.

Sweetly do you and I riff-raff, bask in dance of fire-flies
that crowd a bush from my teen-hood; I feel awkward
        in this balmy night breeze.

Winds of memory singe, hum through my curling hair when
school days and *koyel* songs called to my call… when also shone
        heavy golden pendant sailing pendulous in sky.

I hear far away an ocean going by – *tsunami* waves play
where danger never ceases. Ever.
        Recalling can be dangerous.

I see your lost aching poem crash toss in the wild milky waves –
wee fire-fly lights up piece of sky. Fierce. Careless. Breathless.

And I? I think of everything I could've been but remain
enchanted
by fire-flies hungry for slice of pie… peach, roses, or anything:
      fragment of unwritten poem
      spoon (even cracked) of soul-soup.

Golden Pear: Patience or Penance?

Golden pear is fire-ripened glory
stolen like embers and love kidnapped.

Muse rests — she must bear poems of love
Last season's frost and bit of rain
fed us all but very little. Very very little.

Dreaming rebel, you then lay chained as a thief
though godlike until winter surrendered to your penance.
We shed ice of this season and waited.
No fire warmed our skin or soup shed hunger.

Soon summer thirstily dried our hair, nails, and eyes.
Then to autumn she turned, white sky settling
amid hills, air of wool polyester in rust-ochre burns.

Muses sang in broken verse of stars that fell
from your eyes tight shut — What if they sprang open?
Do you have words about your glorious infamy?
Yes, bring us fire, bring us victuals, push us over world's edge.

But damn your penance, Prometheus! The world is a-smoke!
Your autumnal hands are caked with chaff of harvest
of eons ago. Golden pear you hold tightly on heaving boson
is shriveled and ghostly — let old lies lose.

Godlike-ness must in triple mirrors review. Surely.
Your pen can make winds rustle into quatrains;
can fire breathe them into songs to stir life?

I rest restless beneath your eyelashes:
What is this law? That pulls roots from its skin.

Photo by Ambika Talwar

Sweet Fire Dance of Dissent

~ *after Rilke's "Spanish Dancer"*

She envisioned herself fire dancing
down hallways, a brilliant neural network.

This is what she did this child – dreamed
stories become minuets – worlds whose
wild hair danced like that of savant
sent to scoop world out of slumber –
set it spinning on dance floor
sprinkled with *raagas* of all time.

Dreamed of friends whose wisdom
would filter through cesspool
refresh gardens hit with drought
She dreamed of parks – baby gurgles rising
children with wide eyes of wonder

This she dreamed … Oh yes!

Her hands one day plucked stars
to shine in hair for lover years away;
her eyes pored over parchment
black ink making story of new ages.

Yes, she dreamed her voice carve
poems of ache from sawdust blood wound
of doves whose seeds of peace
dance across the globe: fragrant myrrh rose
peppered with holy ash.

* * *

Yes, My Sweet Fire, she still sings of dissent
whose eyes brew red wine with dregs
Her quick flames race along rising Vindhyas
Her soles cut on broken glass...
she leaves footprints of red velvet hearts.

Ragged earth sprouts marigolds kissed with dew;
Kaleidoscope of rainbows. Warm summer night sky!

Photo by Ambika Talwar

Kindlings...

Fire Woman Goddess of Lakes!
Melt not the land of ice for fear of flood
but preserve waters for drought-time

Fire Woman, walking our lands
bake clay into statues — when you breathe
into them, spring them into life
for the new world arriving

continually like rivers that once flowed
but falter for fear of running dry…

Fire Woman, cool your fire
lest worlds burn up at your feet

But let your ardor simmer through fruits
on trees luscious in the breeze,
through flowers smiling before the wilt

Let your ardor ignite arboreal rhythms
into shade for the resting
where love incandescent glows
in your arms your abundant arms

If the breeze is tropical
or Icelandic it will matter not

This is love that weaves unceasingly
from land to water to air to fire that glows
far in ethers beyond our eyes can see

May all our eyes become love, our arms tinder
we kindling hum mouth to mouth
worlds into being....

Photo by Ambika Talwar

The Waking

Why is it that Sleeping Beloved's dreaming keeps
Beloved awake? That the Open-Eyed Beloved smiles like this?

    fond eyes gazing... melting

While sheets crumple in criss-crossing curves, sky haunts
                    galaxies in longing...

    Why is this? Does anyone know?

Look! An ear of Sleeping One twitches, watching
for words that might be sung aloud, as when no one is watching!

    Especially She,
    when she's not watching.

And the Open-Eyed One is sure no one is listening —

    Especially She.
    Only then will He sing.

Ah! She sighs while her busily sweaty brow
is kissed by a single bee! Signifying fertility.

    How bee buzzes over her hair
    trails over a fallen pillow happy with down
        an angel without wings...

And He watches! Eyes wide hardly blinking or daring to

*...but for joy! His fingers daring
to caress. Do. And his breath... O of air.*

In a split second, She smiles – As if she knows!

*Did you see? How Aurora Borealis reins
in wild hot southern skies....*

Photo by Ambika Talwar

Singularity

I see fire eyes
walk them into water
pools are layered
with desire

rainfall on dirt
makes rivulets

god's tears

2 ~
one touch makes ripples
across the globe

one touch enlivens
one touch destroys

leaves of forget-me-not
close shut when you touch

even a gentle nudge
of finger tip

3 ~
surfaces
  reflect
    project

remind
reveal

sometimes nothing

except when they
are invisible

4 ~
beneath surface
bottomlessness

grabs you
or makes you buoyant
it sings
songs strange to you
unless
you shut your ears

then you smile

5 ~
then you weep
fill the bowls

that will reflect
changing sky

where flowers float

if the bowl were a trough
horses would drink

from them lovingly

6 ~
now birds hop
on walls of bowl

skim the still and circling
surface

for a draft of patience
sustenance

amrita
is this: nothing else

7 ~
first you must learn
how to stand in fire

as Sita
who did not burn

but revealed her purity
left the home
that doubted her
first you must learn
how to dance in fire

transform worlds
fearlessly

beyond reprisal
All One Is!

8 ~
there is a friend
Nameless one
Guide Beloved

who won't cast stones
but clear the way

know you her?

9 ~
fire is born in water

this is how life generates
itself: *Metta*

#

amrita: Skt. manna of immortality. Mrityu means death. Amrit means immortal.

Sita: In the Indian epic *Ramayana*, Sita, in exile with her beloved Rama, is abducted by Ravana. Refusing to enter his home, Sita stays in his garden until Rama brings his army to rescue her. Victorious, they return to their Ayodhya, but people doubt her purity. She takes the fire test of purity and survives. She chooses to leave Rama for doubting her.

Metta: compassion

Maja and Ambika in Pasadena, February 2016

Photo by Ambika Talwar

Love: Salt of the Earth

We are the salt of the earth ... so some say
we taste ourselves in our tears
we wish these be tears of love
or why waste the wellspring of our eyes
even morning sun breathes through
morning water eyes shining through the window
as its light spreads incandescent
over a hushed sleeping city.
* * *

Good morning !
* * *

Yes we are salt of the earth
even when day is done
wings of evening begin to spread
organs play their paean through the furrows
taste of kisses brings us home
this is how morning sun comes to rest
 cleaving us to our arms interwoven
the salt of you in my mouth
I smell what you have endured
thoughts that make you wondrous
all your toiling peppered with knowing
darkness of night leaves salt hills on the beach
our sweat salts our sheets — taste of comfort
that nothing else creates. Not breakfast.

But something like this. That we awake
always to this melt always to this
smile nose to cheek always to this

salt of the earth with wings
when sun sultry returns winking
through filigree of our fingers
that will spread nimbly to make new things
even to fashion flour, salt, and water
into nourishment with mulled wine…

If this isn't love, what is?
that our skins be woven together
salt sweat smiles tears … you are food
to me as are my dreams.

Photo by Ambika Talwar

Fragrance of Prayer

I like thurible
from which smoke escapes
as fragrance from flower
upside down
lit with a thousand lights
as One

itself a psalm
it courses its way through
tensed waking morning air
into jeweled hearts
that know a prayer
unheard — is a prayer
whose silence

changes worlds
as golden bell of ancient ones
in far distance of heart
wears the robe
of fortitude:
old flower remembers
her presence is prayer

her womb a crucible
of infinite birthing.

Maja Trochimczyk

Selfie in Paris, 2014

Why, Write?

My self-introduction as a poet on my website opens with a statement: "Poetry is a way of life and a shortcut to the sublime..." An avid reader of poetry since my Polish childhood, I started writing in English after I emigrated to Canada and lost the ground under my feet — my family, language, culture... Yet, my loss became my gain, when I created a new family, found a new language, and discovered a new culture to contribute to in this New World of English. Indeed, to quote my old essay, "the flexibility, richness and focus of this language never cease to amaze me!" Writing in English is also helpful in creating a new identity: it is all "persona" writing as I try on my different poetic hats, and look in the mirror of words to see if I'm an Exile or a Queen.

Since 1995, I have kept a personal poetic journal and gave all sorts of poems to my friends. I like illustrating them with my photographs, taken mostly in my garden and neighborhood of Southern California. In 2006, I decided to share my work at public readings and in publications, .I continued to write short poems, in a genre I called "freeway poetry" — composed in my head while commuting, and committed to paper upon arrival. In 2010, I was selected to serve as the Sixth Poet Laureate of Sunland Tujunga; it still is my favorite title and I continue volunteering to promote poetry in my neighborhood, organize readings, and publish.

In the same year, thanks to the poetry anthology that I edited to celebrate Chopin's bicentennial, *Chopin with Cherries*, I met Millicent, Kathi, and Georgia who all submitted beautiful work for this romantic anthology. Joining the WWW group was the next logical next step. We have shared our poetic discoveries and fascinations ever since; we have helped each other grow. Having to bring a new poem each month was sometimes a challenge, but mostly a joy of sharing and learning.

Personally, I never considered poetry a "career." I'm already a musicologist (Ph.D.) and a grant writer; I do not need to make poetry into a job! Thus, I have avoided competitions and conferences, and initially wrote only for myself. Meanwhile, I discovered that having a roomful of people wait with bated breath for my next word was and is completely addictive. And the shortest way to finding myself in front of such an awe-struck audience is to workshop my poems with really talented poets.

In the following selections from 20 years of poetry-writing, I included self-portraits as an émigré, daughter, and lover, and a poem I wrote for Millicent, grateful for her charming and eccentric home with a rustic patio - daffodils in the spring, red-white-and-blue lanterns in the summer, and gold leaves in the autumn. Include in my self-portrait a "responsorial" poem from my *Into Light* book of spiritually inspired verse and incantations. Over the years, I wrote a lot of dirges and plaints; in this book, I gathered my positive, inspirational poems. It is time to think of what I'll leave behind and those types of poems are my little treasures to be shared with children and friends.

For me, poetry writing truly is about "Grateful Conversations" — with myself, with my friends, with the world... I am deeply thankful for the ten years and many hours of conversing with Westside Women Writers!

~ **Maja Trochimczyk**

Definition: Writing

~ *in response to George Jisho Robertson's
essay "Path of Poesis"*

It is not like splitting the match in four
or counting devils on its round head —
none of this matters, really

see the sunrise above Strawberry Peak
and Mount Disappointment shimmer
on the puffy underbelly of summer clouds

be dazed by bright ripples on a shallow canyon stream
shining like scales of a carp waiting to be killed
in a bathtub before Polish Easter

listen to the roosting birds at dusk,
the murder of crows covering tree branches
with angular shapes, dense Xenakis chords,

black clusters, dissonant, intense. They bathe
in the river, sit on a concrete bank with wet wings
outstretched, drooping with water, docile

like tattooed crowds resting, sweating
on sandy beach towels in Santa Monica,
waiting for a *tsunami* that will not come

shifting the gaze is important, from the navel
to cosmos — not how we fail in a multitude of ways,
but what graces hide in galaxies

that collide amidst exploding supernovas,
on thousands of inhabitable planets
we'll count but never touch –

we'll touch but never count
the veins on the petals of the rose
shriveling from desert heat, just opened

Not us, then, look around, beyond,
catch what's already gone, hold it
in your hand — the spark, the passing

Photo by Maja Trochimczyk

In Millicent's World

~ for my friend, Millicent Borges Accardi

Round paper balls of stars and stripes shine
between white flowers on a Mirabelle plum tree
above thick planks of wooden table on the patio.

Daffodils spill over from flower beds into vibrant patches
of sunny yellow among dried, crumbling leaves
under the canopy of live oaks in her Topanga garden.

No, it is not the Fourth of July, here's a different kind
of freedom, tasted in the lightness of *vinho verde*
heard in the phrases of a mocking bird

that amuses us with a thousand melodies
of other birds, while we read our poems,
sparkling with the colors of India, Serbia, Poland,

the dust of Oklahoma, the sharp hospital lights
in a cancer ward — *will he live?* — moonlight between
pine branches swaying above the surface of a lake,

dew drops in the misty *laurisilva* of Madeira, the softness
of Portuguese on her tongue, as she retells folk-tales
that end badly — the beauty that slept in and killed the beast

love that could not be mentioned, ghosts in the machine,
stories, poems, stories — *this is what people do*, she says
they do not answer their phone unless it rings twice, times eight

a thousand words, blessings above the stream
flowing through her overgrown garden, the world
in a translucent green glass served by Millicent, the poet.

An Ode of the Lost

~ *to Adam Mickiewicz and all Polish exiles*

Tired exiles in rainy Paris listen to Mickiewicz
reciting praises of woodsy hills, green meadows —
distant Lithuania, their home painted in Polish verse,
each word thickly spread with meaning,
like a slice of rye bread with buckwheat honey.

"*Litwo! Ojczyzno moja! ty jesteś jak zdrowie.*
Ile cię trzeba cenić, ten tylko się dowie,
Kto cię stracił" — he says, and we, homeless Poles
without ground under our feet, concur,
sharing the blame for our departure.
There's no return.

Are not all journeys one way? Forward,
forward, go on, "*call that going, call that on.*"
The speed of light, merciless angel with a flaming sword,
moves the arrow forward. Seconds, minutes
stretch into years. Onwards. Go.
The time-space cone limits the realm of possibility.
If you stay, you can go on. If you leave —

Can you find blessing in the blur of a moment?
In a glimpse of soft, grassy slopes shining
like burnished gold before the sun turns purple?
Can you learn to love the sweet-fluted songs
of the mockingbird, forget the nightingale?

How far is too far for the lost country
to become but a dream of ancient kings —
where children never cry, wildflowers bloom,
and autumn flutter of brown, drying leaves
whispers of the comforts of winter?

*Sleep, sleep, eternal sleep,
in the spring you will awaken...*

Photo by Maja Trochimczyk

NOTE: Quotation in Polish ("My country! You are as good health: How much one should prize you, he only can tell who has lost you") is from the national epic, Adam Mickiewicz's *Invocation to Pan Tadeusz, or the Last Foray in Lithuania*. The second quotation is from Samuel Beckett's *The Unnamable*.

On Eating a Donut at the Kraków Airport

I am moved to tears by the taste of a donut
Polish donut at a Kraków airport

Puffy, oval, brown yeast ball with sticky white icing
of *lukier*, dotted with candied orange peel

And the aroma of the rose *confiture*, a delight
I found in a café with a pretentious English name

One "Morning Coffee" in an ancient city of a hundred
Kawiarnias — alive with the dark fragrance of *kawa*

That black powder looted from the Turkish army
After the victory of Polish cavalry ended the siege of Vienna

Ah, forgotten stories, secrets, tastes of my childhood
My mom's gifts and lessons how to properly peel an orange

Cook slices in syrup, add just enough vodka to the dough
To keep grease away... I bite into the soft, white flesh

My eyes fill with tears I had swallowed
When I walked into her antique-filled condo

And I saw her — frail, dove-white, forgetful
A shadow of the boisterous woman I feared

She ruled over her family with iron resolve
And made perfect donuts with rosehips and orange

I cry over my donut on this cloudy morning
Grey Polish skies open to let sunrays through

A dazzling hole in heaven, like the triangular eye
Of the Trinity resting on a stack of puffy clouds

On the ceiling of the Baroque church on Skałka
The nation's shrine with gold angels on sandstone walls

It saw generations pass on their pilgrimage
To the agate-columned altar and the eye of infinity

This Divine Eye looks at me from beyond
when I bite into the teary saltiness of my donut

Sweet Polish donut at a Kraków airport —
Full, round donut as it should be

NOTE: Polish words; "Lukier" = icing, "kawa"=coffee, "kawiarnia" = café..

Shambhala

~ for Polish families deported by Soviets to Siberia in 1940.

Do children who die on the way
carry bejeweled parasols in a Tibetan heaven?

Is Siberia too far from Shambhala
for the bedraggled orphans to enter through
its golden doorways, glistening with ten thousand
ornaments, treasures from a galaxy with ten billion suns?

Are they too sick and dirty to walk on a shining path
made for the birth of the Buddha — scented
with sandalwood, adorned with an unsurpassed
multitude of rarest gems.

When the Buddha was born, the Earth
moved six ways, the wise man said.

Did it move at least once to mark your passage?

When you rolled in pain and moaned
until the blessed moment of relief?
Gave up your last breath like a crystal question mark
in a frozen Siberian air? Convulsed
in a sudden burst of gunfire, a bullet straight
through your heart? Froze to death in a convoy?
Fainted on the floor of a railroad car?

There was no hooting of owls, they say,
when the great Shakyamuni Buddha
was born. Sweet-sounding music floated

through a myriad of flowering orchards,
filled with a rainbow of gemstone trees.

Did you hear an owl hoot when you died?

Oh, hungry child of gulags, the lost child
of Siberia — Did the Earth move?

Were there parasols, or owls?

Photo by Maja Trochimczyk

The Lady with an Ermine

*~ after Leonardo da Vinci's portrait of Cecilia Gallerani,
from the Czartoryski Museum in Cracow*

Her gaze follows me around the room
She shares that secretive smile with her famous cousin.
Filled with knowledge of what was, what will be,
she slowly caresses the smooth, warm ermine fur.

Tesoro, amore mio, sii tranquillo , ti amo

Leonardo's brush made a space for her to inhabit,
a grey-blue sky was painted black much later –
she was pregnant, her son – a Sforza bastard,
the white ermine – the emblem of her Duke.

Sheltered by Polish royalty, she revealed
her charms only to their closest confidantes.
In 1830, exiled, in a box of precious wood, to Paris.
In 1919, returned, to taste Polish freedom.

amore mio, sii tranquillo , ti amo

In 1939 hidden again, found by Germans
For Hitler's last dream, Linz *Führermuseum*
Art among red flags and swastikas, flourishing
in the dark cavern of his mind. Never built.

From Berlin to occupied Kraków, to Governor Frank's
hunting lodge in Bavaria… The Red Army was closing in.

The swastikas gone, in crisp winter air, American soldiers
held her tight for the cameras of Monument Men.

sii tranquillo , ti amo

Back home in Kraków she is safe in the navy recess
of a museum wall, under muted spotlight. Children
play a game: *Walk briskly from right to left, don't
let your eyes leave her eyes, see how she is watching you.*

Her gaze follows me around the room
Filled with knowledge of what was, what will be,
she slowly caresses the smooth, warm ermine fur.
She knows that I know that she knows.

amore mio, ti amo

* NOTE: "Tesoro, amore mio, sii tranquillo, tiamo" – "Sweetheart, my love, be quiet, I love you" – a fragment of a love letter in Italian.

On Divine Comedy and Ice-Cream

My Muse has chocolate eyes and a goatee.
Disabled by grief, he looks for me in the dark,
touching. His hands outline the contour
of my hips as he sighs and says "that's right"
in this deep baritone of his, the sweetest of voices.

What next? I wonder as we sit on the leather sofa
sticky in the heat, eat almonds and ice cream
with milk, watch silly comedies about aliens
and time machines, friends *being excellent
to each other*, playing air guitar. We leaf through
the other Comedy, the Divine one:
Il Paradiso as seen by Giovanni di Paolo.
Medieval illuminations for the end of time.

Submerged in the Earth's shadow, the Moon sphere
is the haven for the likes of us, inconstant,
waxing and waning, not keeping their vows.

Dante and Beatrix, the poet and his beloved,
rise up to Mercury of the ambitious and Venus
of lovers, the Garden of Earthly Delights
where we stay as they ascend from the Fourth Sphere
of the Sun through the Eight of Fixed Stars,
to meet the wise, the virtuous, martyrs,
saints, the multitude of angels in Primum Mobile
and the blessed, don't forget the blessed
of the Tenth Sphere, the divine Empyrean —

The heart of Paradise where gold rays of light
always permeate everything, where saints
sleep in rose petal pods, like babies by their mothers,
or splash in and out of the waters of grace, the river
of serenity that flows under the buzzing of heavenly bees,
making timeless honey — sweet, translucent, gold honey,
only honey, forever and beyond time, honey —

Photo by Maja Trochimczyk

Repeat After Me

> ~ *after Prayer for Fukushima Waters by Dr. Masaru Emoto:*
> *Water, we are sorry /*
> *Water, please forgive us /*
> *Water, we thank you /*
> *Water, we love you*

Yes, you can find it. / Your way out. /
It is so simple. / First you say: /

I AM SORRY / – WE ARE SO SORRY. /

We are the guilty ones, / we are all at fault! /

What happens next? / The door opens. /
We stop at the threshold and say: /

PLEASE FORGIVE ME, / I FORGIVE YOU. /

Forgiveness erases / all my fears, /
all our sorrows / The burden
of dead thoughts is lifted. / See? /

We float up into brightness. /
We are sparks of starlight. /
a constellation dancing in the sky /
as we say: /

THANK YOU, / THANK YOU VERY MUCH. /

Filled with gratitude /
for every cloud, leaf and petal, /
every breath we take,/ every heartbeat,/
we are ready, at last,/
to say what's the most important:/

I LOVE YOU, MY WORLD, /
I LOVE YOU, MY SUNLIGHT /

I give you all the love /
of my tired, grateful heart!/

That's right, let's say it again./

I LOVE YOU,MY SPLENDID, STUPENDOUS,
EXQUISITE, DELIGHTFULAND MAGNIFICENT LIFE!

Now, step by step,
one word at a time...

*NOTE: Each phrase to be recited by the reader
and repeated by the listeners at the / sign.*

In Morning Light

We live on a planet where it rains diamonds —
hard rain, sparkling crystal droplets — in the clouds,
in the air, on the ground under our feet.

Here, the Valentine's Day falls on Ash Wednesday.
Red strawberries, wine-hot passion and *Ashes to ashes,
dust to dust* — lessons of impermanence of the body,
constantly reconfigured in a vortex of quarks and atoms
until the pattern dissolves like snow at the end of winter.
Delicate snowdrops peek from under the melting cover
of phantasmagorical shapes and figures.

Here, the Annunciation Day of Mary's greatest joy
falls on Palm Sunday — from rainbow wings of Fra Angelico's
Gabriel bowing before the shy, blushing maiden in royal blue
we look ahead to the green of palm fronds lining the streets
of Jerusalem. We welcome the destiny of the King.
We see red blood on the stones of Golgotha,
the Place of the Skull. Not even this is real.

No wonder, then, that Easter, the greatest Mystery —
of Death into Life, Spirit over Matter, the Divine
in an emptied human shell — *Eli, Eli, Lema Sabachthani* —
Sanctus, Benedictus, Agnus Dei — *it is done* —
yes, that Easter — is on April's Fools Day this year.

We fool ourselves when we see death as enemy.
We spin our lives into thin filaments of a spider-web.
Illusion woven into illusion. Deception after deception.
They rise and fall with the rhythm of seductive charm.

The smiling demon is the most persistent. Incorrigible,
it pulls us down, down, down into the mud,
from whence we did *not* come. Nothingness
ties us up with bonds of non-belonging.

My revelation is this — we live on the planet
where it rains diamonds. We walk on untold treasures
that we do not notice — we forget and forget and forget
where we came from, where we are, where we are going.
We spin our future out of spider silk and shadows.
Our lives fill with the sand of dreams, changing
like shards of glass, broken bits of colored plastic
in a kaleidoscope — transfigured into the most
astounding waltz of the rosettes, reflected
in hexagonal mirrors of transcendence —

My revelation is this — we are the children
of Sunlight — blessed by Radiance — wearing
Love's golden halos — we shine and blossom —
in Light's cosmic garden of stars — lilies — violets —
peonies — daffodils — and roses — always roses —
in this brilliant garden — on a diamond planet —
of what is — *in the Heart of the Great, Great Silence* —

— there's no here — nor there —
— no before — nor after —
— no inside — nor outside —

— — — All is Always Now — — —
— — — All is Always One — — —
— — — Where We Are — — —

NOTE: References to the Gospels, Giordano Bruno, and St. Germain.

Photo by Maja Trochimczyk

Biographies

WWW poets without Georgia and Madeleine at a Topanga Canyon workshop, March 2018. L to R: Susan, Lois, Sonya, Ambika, Kathi and Millicent. Maja in the center in the back.

MILLICENT BORGES ACCARDI, a Portuguese-American writer, is the author of four poetry books, most recently *Only More So* (Salmon Poetry). Her awards include fellowships from the National Endowment for the Arts (NEA), Fulbright, Canto Mundo, Creative Capacity, the California Arts Council, Fundação Luso-Americana, and Barbara Deming Foundation. She's led poetry workshops at Keystone College, Nimrod Writers Conference, The Muse in Norfolk, Virginia, and University of Texas, Austin. Her non-fiction can be found in *The Writers Chronicle, Poets Quarterly,* and the *Portuguese American Journal*. Recent readings at Brown University, Rutgers, UMass Dartmouth, Rhode Island College and the Carr Series at the University of Illinois, Champaign/Urbana

MADELEINE S. BUTCHER has been writing since 1979. An actress at that time, she wrote monologues, scenes and plays, later transitioning to short stories, guided by Merrill Joan Gerber. Poetry was always cropping up on its own, from time to time. She is a graduate of NYU School of the Arts with a BFA in dance and has performed off Broadway and on. She has taught ballet to toddlers, teenagers and adults. She taught playwriting, modern dance, ballet and improvisation to at risk youth. Besides dance and acting, she worked as an assistant picture and sound editor on features for sixteen years. She taught Pilates out of her home studio for ten years in Woodland Hills. She has been a member of Westside Women Writers for three years. Her first piece was published in the *West Marin Journal*, 2015. She and her husband are retired, traveling and hoping to settle on San Juan Island in the great state of Washington.

GEORGIA JONES-DAVIS grew up in Northern New Mexico and Southern California. She worked as Assistant Book Review Editor for *The Los Angeles Herald Examiner* and *The Los Angeles Times*. She has contributed to *The Washington Post, The Philadelphia Inquirer, The Chicago Tribune, Salon magazine, New Mexico Magazine, South West Book Views* and other publications. A former board member of Valley Contemporary Poets, a Southern California non-profit, Georgia was honored as one of the 2010 Newer Poets by the Los Angeles Poetry Festival and the Los Angeles Public Library ALOUD series. Her work has appeared in *West Wind, The California Quarterly, Brevities, The Bicycle Review, Nebo, Eclipse, poetic diversity,* Sam Hamil's online zine, *Poets Against War, Ascent Aspirations* and *South Bank Poetry, London.*

She has new work soon to appear in *The Serving House Journal*. Georgia is the author of two chapbooks, *Blue Poodle* 2011) and *Night School*, (2015), both published by Finishing Line Press. Georgia Jones-Davis lives in Santa Fe, New Mexico, where she writes, hikes with her dog, and loves the changing light on the Sangre de Cristo and Jemez Mountains.

LOIS P. JONES is a recipient of the 2016 Bristol Poetry Prize and the 2012 Tiferet Poetry Prize. Her work has been published in anthologies including *The Poet's Quest for God* (Eyewear Publishing), *Wide Awake: Poetry of Los Angeles and Beyond* (The Pacific Coast Poetry Series), *30 Days* (Tupelo Press) and *Good-Bye Mexico* (Texas Review Press), and many journals including *Narrative, American Poetry Journal, Tupelo Quarterly, The Warwick Review, Cider Press Review* and others. Lois was shortlisted for the 2016 Bridport Prize in poetry. She is Poetry Editor of Kyoto Journal, host of KPFK's Poets Café (Pacifica Radio) and co-hosts Moonday Poetry. Her first poetry collection, *Night Ladder*, has been recently released by Glass Lyre Press.

SUSAN ROGERS considers poetry a vehicle for light. She is a practitioner of Sukyo Mahikari—a spiritual practice promoting positivity. She is also a licensed attorney and artist. She received her Masters in Creative Writing from Johns Hopkins University following her Juris Doctor from UCLA Law and her BA in English Literature from Princeton University. She has taught Creative Writing at Johns Hopkins University and given lectures in English Literature at UCLA. Her poetry is included in numerous anthologies and journals including Altadena Poetry Review, California Quarterly, Carrying the Branch: *Poets in Search of Peace, Kyoto Journal, Light on Light Magazine. Meditations on Divine Names, Pirene's Fountain, Saint Julian's Press, San Diego Poetry Annual: The Best Poems of San Diego* and *Tiferet Journal*. She was Writer of the Week for "Words, Spirit and You," sponsored by *Tiferet Journal*. One of her haiku won Honorable Mention in the 2010 Kiyoshi and Kiyoko Tokutomi Memorial Haiku Contest. She has featured at poetry reading series including Moonday Poetry, Bolton Hall Museum and Rapp Saloon. She has also shared her poetry at universities, museums, art galleries, environmental conferences and workshops for youth recovering from substance addiction. She was interviewed for KPFK's Poet's Café archived at www.timothy-green.org/blog/susan-rogers. She was nominated for a Pushcart Prize in 2013 and 2017. Her poem "The Origin is One" was performed at the

televised Akigami Ice Festival in Gifu, Japan. Watch the short film made from this poem at
https://www.youtube.com/watch?v=rzPA9zeC0Qc.

SONYA SABANAC (neé Zivic) was born and raised in Former Yugoslavia, a country that no longer exists. Disappeared like Atlántida and left its former citizens to carry a heavy burden of constant search for a home. Sonya was born in the City of Sarajevo, where she graduated from Sarajevo University School of Law. In the midst of the war that made her country gone, in 1992, Sonya left the county with her family and spent two years in Denmark living as a refugee. She immigrated into USA in 1994, and landed at Los Angeles, where she still lives. She was a passionate reader all her life and an ardent poetry lover, but she only started writing in her late forties. Sonya is a member of Los Angeles Westside Women Writers Group. Her poems appeared in *San Gabriel Valley Poetry Quarterly, Magnapoets, Poetic Diversity* and the anthology about Immigrant Women *Shifting Balance Sheets* that also published her memoir, *How I Decided to Go a Little Crazy*. In addition to writing, Sonya is also a photographer. She has many projects in store; one of them is to publish a book that will connect short stories with her photo images.

KATHI STAFFORD graduated from the Masters in Professional Writing program at the University of Southern California with a poetry concentration. Her poetry, book reviews, and interviews have appeared in many journals, such as *Rattle, Hiram Poetry Review, Connecticut River Review, Chiron Review, Nerve Cowboy,* and *Southern California Review.* Her poetry has been anthologized in *Chopin and Cherries* and *Sea of Alone: Poems for Hitchcock.* She is a former editor of the *Southern California Review* and her "day job" background is as a corporate attorney. Her first book, *Blank Check* (Finishing Line Press), was released in 2016.

AMBIKA TALWAR is an educator, poet and artist, who has composed poems since her teen years. She has authored and self-published *Creative Resonance: Poetry — Elegant Play, Elegant Change; 4 Stars & 25 Roses* (poems for her father) and, more recently, *My Greece: Mirrors & Metamorphoses,* a poetic biographical spiritual journey through Greece. She is published in *Kyoto Journal; Inkwater Ink, vol. 3;* Moonrise Press anthologies *(Chopin with Cherries, Meditations on Divine*

Names), *VIA, Poets on Site* collections, the *Tower Journal, St. Julian's Press, Life & Legends,* and others. Interviewed by KPFK, she also won an award in Belgium for a short film. Her ecstatic writing style makes her poetry a "bridge to other worlds." She resides in Los Angeles/New Delhi, practices energy medicine, and teaches at Cypress College, California. She believes it is through our creativity that we gain self-knowledge and become activators of change.
creativeinfinities.com, goldenmatrixvisions.com

MAJA TROCHIMCZYK, Ph.D., is a Polish American poet, music historian, photographer, and author of seven books of poetry, including: *Miriam's Iris* (2008), *Slicing the Bread* (2014), *The Rainy Bread* (2016), *Into Light* (2016), and two anthologies, *Chopin with Cherries* (2010) and *Meditations on Divine Names* (2012). Her poems appeared in such journals as the *California Quarterly, Cosmopolitan Review, Ekphrasis Journal, Epiphany Magazine, Lily Literary Review, Loch Raven Review, Lummox Journal, Quill and Parchment, Pirene's Fountain, Poezja Dzisiaj, The Scream Online, Spectrum.* Her work was also included in anthologies by Poets on Site, Southern California Haiku Study Group, and others. As a Polish music historian, she published seven books, most recently *Górecki in Context: Essays on Music* (2017) and *Frédéric Chopin: A Research and Information Guide* (rev. ed., 2015). A former Poet Laureate of Sunland-Tujunga, she is the founder of Moonrise Press, Board Secretary of the Polish American Historical Association, and President of Helena Modjeska Culture Club. Her research studies, articles and book chapters appeared in English, Polish, and in translations in ten countries. She read papers at over 80 international conferences and is a recipient of honors and awards from Polish, Canadian, and American institutions, such as the American Council of Learned Societies, the Polish Ministry of Culture, PAHA, McGill University, and the University of Southern California. Two solo exhibitions displayed her photographs of leaves and roses.
trochimczyk.net, moonrisepress.com, poetrylaurels.blogspot.com.

Future WWW at *Chopin with Cherries* reading, May 2010, with Marian Kaplun Shapiro. L to R: Georgia, Maja, Ambika, Susan and Millicent.

Madeleine and Millicent at the Norton Simon Museum, 2013.

Maja, Georgia, and Lisa Cheby featured poets presenting their new books at Beyond Baroque, Venice, 2015.

Lois, Ambika, Kathi, Maja and Susan after Lois's featured reading at Bolton Hall Museum, Tujunga, August 2017.